VISUAL QUICKSTART GUIDE

iCHAT AV 2

FOR MAC OS X

Jeff Carlson

Peachpit Press

Visual QuickStart Guide
iChat AV 2 for Mac OS X
Jeff Carlson

Peachpit Press

1249 Eighth Street
Berkeley, CA 94710
(800) 283-9444, (510) 524-2178, (510) 524-2221 (fax)

Find us on the World Wide Web at: www.peachpit.com
To report errors, please send a note to errata@peachpit.com
Peachpit Press is a division of Pearson Education

Editor: Nancy Davis
Copyeditor: Agen G. N. Schmitz
Production Editor: Lisa Brazieal
Composition: Jeff Carlson
Cover Design: The Visual Group
Cover Production: George Mattingly / GMD
Indexer: Caroline Parks, Indexcellence

ISBN: 0-321-23773-0

9 8 7 6 5 4 3 2 1

Printed and bound in the United States of America

Dedication

For Jessica, whose chats I will greatly miss.

Special Thanks to

Nancy Davis, for crowding me into her unbelievable schedule and keeping my enthusiasm high.

Agen G. N. Schmitz, for his keen eyes, exceptional music recommendations, and for rejoining the fold.

Lisa Brazieal, for production assistance and being my iChat guinea pig at times.

Caroline Parks, for continuing to say yes, despite the schedule.

Stefan Offerman and **Keri Walker,** for answering my questions and providing the tools I needed.

Glenn Fleishman, David Blatner, Steve Roth, Jeff Tolbert, and **Laurence Chen,** for support, advice, and stress relief, and **Brigette Schaffarzick** for the oatmeal chocolate chip cookies.

Dave, Steve, Heather, Kai, and the rest of the gang at **Diva Espresso,** for oh-so-many double-tall lattés and Americanos.

Kim Carlson, for 10-plus years of joy.

TABLE OF CONTENTS

Introduction   **vii**

Chapter 1: iChat AV Overview   **1**
iChat AV System Requirements 2
A Tour of iChat's Interface 4
Getting Connected 6

Chapter 2: Creating Your iChat Persona   **9**
Obtaining a Screen Name 10
Creating Your Persona 11
Setting Your Status 12
Customizing the Status Message 14
Changing Your Text Appearance 16
Setting the Chat Background 18
Configuring Alerts 20
Switching to Another Account 22
Logging In and Out 23
Setting Your Privacy Level 24

Chapter 3: Your Buddy Icon   **25**
Importing Images 26
Taking a Video Capture 28
Making Better Buddy Icons 29
Using Multiple Buddy Icons 30

Chapter 4: The Buddy List   **31**
Adding Buddies 32
iChat and Address Book 36
Customizing the Buddy List Display 38
Viewing More Buddy Information 40
Setting Buddy Actions 42
Managing Buddy Groups 44
Adding a Buddy to a Group 45

Chapter 5: Text Chat   **47**
Initiating a Text Chat 48
Receiving a Text Chat 51
Blocking a Person 52
Text Chat in Groups 54

Public Group Chats 57
Checking Spelling 58
Inserting Smileys 60
Adding Hyperlinks 61
Sending and Receiving Images 62
Changing Text Formatting 63
Changing Message Appearance 64
Reformatting Incoming Messages 65
Working with Chat Transcripts 66

Chapter 6: Audio Chat 69
Preparing for an Audio Chat 70
Starting an Audio Chat 71
Starting a One-Way Audio Chat 74
Receiving an Audio Chat 75
Muting Audio 76
Using the Connection Doctor 77

Chapter 7: Video Chat 79
Preparing for a Video Chat 80
Previewing Your Video Image 82
Starting a Video Chat 83
Starting a One-Way Video Chat 85
Receiving a Video Chat 86
Resizing the Video Window 87
Muting and Pausing a Video Chat 88
Arranging the Preview Image 89
Taking a Snapshot of a Video Chat 90
Setting Bandwidth Limit 91

Chapter 8: Mail and File Transfer 93
Sending Email from iChat 94
Checking Buddy Availability in Mail 96
Starting a Chat from within Mail 97
Transferring a File 98
Receiving a File 99

Appendix A: Troubleshooting 101
Lost or Failed Connections 102

Appendix B: Customizing iChat AV 105
Customizing iChat 106

Index 109

INTRODUCTION

When I first told people I was writing a book about Apple's iChat AV, I received furrowed brows and puzzled looks. Would it be a pamphlet? What's there to write about? After all, iChat AV is a simple application, sending little text messages from one person's computer to another. Right?

Sure. Unless you're participating in a group chat, where everyone sees all the messages. Or doing audio and video conferencing, which are cool and often productive. Or sending images and other files from one person to another—well, it also previews PDF files, which is also pretty cool when you think about it. And then, of course, iChat AV tells you when your friends are online, even when you're using a different program like Apple's Mail or Address Book, which means you're not wasting time composing email messages when a simple two-minute chat would answer your questions, and...

You can see where this is going. iChat is a simple application, but one that illustrates exactly why millions of Mac users have adopted it: it seems basic on the surface, but offers a surprising amount of depth.

This book reveals that depth, from setting up your screen name to videoconferencing across the globe. You'll soon realize that there's plenty to chat about.

iCHAT AV OVERVIEW

Online chatting isn't new, and it isn't new to the Macintosh, either—AOL subscribers have been able to chat with each other for years, and there are also software clients that tie into IRC (Internet Relay Chat) and Microsoft's MSN network. However, iChat AV makes it seem as if you've discovered chatting because its implementation is so good. Once again, Apple has looked at a product and asked, "What do people really want?" The answer, which should come as no surprise, was a chat client that is simple to use, easy to read, and devoid of annoying ads or gimmicks.

This chapter introduces iChat AV—what you need to use it, and what it can do. I also cover the two types of networking that iChat offers: across the Internet using AIM (AOL Instant Messenger) and on a local network using Rendezvous networking.

iChat AV System Requirements

Despite its apparent simplicity, iChat AV is a sophisticated networking client that sometimes has stiff system requirements depending on what you want it to do. Text chatting, for example, doesn't require much processing overhead, but video conferencing can easily push your Mac to its limits.

iChat AV is included with Mac OS X 10.3 Panther; if you're still using Jaguar, you can purchase iChat AV from Apple for $30. The following are Apple's requirements. See Chapters 5, 6, and 7 for details on each type of chat.

Text chat requirements

◆ Macintosh computer with a PowerPC G3, G4, or G5 processor

◆ Mac OS X 10.2.5 Jaguar (Mac OS X 10.2.8 or later and QuickTime 6.4 recommended)

◆ Internet connection (no minimum speed)

Audio chat requirements

◆ Macintosh computer with a PowerPC G3, G4, or G5 processor

◆ Mac OS X 10.2.5 Jaguar (Mac OS X 10.2.8 or later and QuickTime 6.4 recommended)

◆ An internal or external microphone

◆ Internet connection with a speed of at least a 56 Kbps modem

Video chat requirements

◆ Macintosh computer with a PowerPC G3, G4, or G5 processor running at 600 MHz or faster

◆ Mac OS X 10.2.5 Jaguar (Mac OS X 10.2.8 or later and QuickTime 6.4 recommended)

◆ iSight (which has a built-in microphone) or an internal or external microphone for audio

◆ iSight or any FireWire-based video camera for video (DV camcorders require a G4 or G5 processor)

◆ Internet connection with a speed of at least 100 Kbps or faster (Cable, DSL, or other broadband)

iChat versus iChat AV

iChat AV is actually the second version of iChat. iChat 1.0 offered text messaging and file transfer. You can still get iChat 1.0 as part of Mac OS X 10.2 Jaguar.

Instead of spending the entire book pointing out differences between the two programs, I focus on iChat AV exclusively. However, most of the material in this book related to creating accounts and text chatting applies to iChat 1.0 as well.

So, throughout the book I'll refer to iChat AV as simply "iChat," because it's easier than tacking on "AV" each time, and because you know what I'm talking about.

iChat AV System Requirements

A Tour of iChat's Interface

iChat's interface is the model of simplicity—there are no extraneous buttons, no banner advertisements, no scrolling stock tickers, or any of the other cruft that makes using other chat programs annoying. Following are the main sections of iChat.

Buddy List

The Buddy List is iChat's main window, listing the people with whom you can chat plus controls for initiating chat sessions (**Figure 1.1**). See Chapters 2, 3, and 4 for information on how to manage instant messaging accounts and your Buddy List.

Text chat window

A text chat is a conversation between two or more people using typed words. When you type something and press Return, your message appears in the chat window where everyone involved in the chat can read it (**Figure 1.2**). Chapter 5 goes into greater detail about using text chats.

Audio chat window

If you want to talk about a sparse interface, look at the audio chat window (**Figure 1.3**). The horizontal indicator lights reflect the audio level. The volume slider makes incoming audio louder or softer. And the lone button in this window mutes the connection without ending the chat. See Chapter 6 for more information.

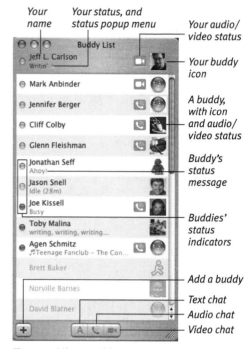

Figure 1.1 iChat's Buddy List shows you who is online.

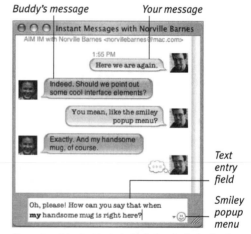

Figure 1.2 A typical text chat window includes back-and-forth messages, like in real conversation.

A TOUR OF ICHAT'S INTERFACE

Mute button *Audio level indicator*

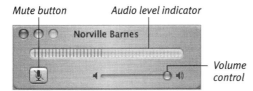

Figure 1.3 The audio chat window is understandably sparse.

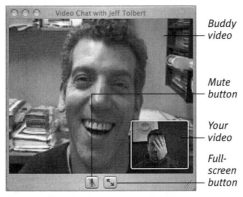

Buddy video

Mute button

Your video

Full-screen button

Figure 1.4 A video chat includes the video feed from your buddy, as well as the video of you that he sees.

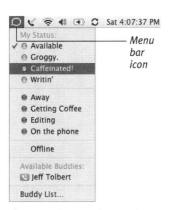

Menu bar icon

Figure 1.5 The menu bar icon is a quick way to change your status.

Mac OS X Dock

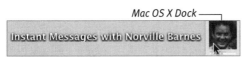

Figure 1.6 Text chat windows minimize to display the other person's buddy icon in the Dock.

Video chat window

The bulk of the video chat window is occupied by the image of the person you're chatting with (**Figure 1.4**). A smaller, resizable window receives the feed from your camera and displays what the other person is seeing. The only other visible controls here are a button to pause and mute the video stream and a button to switch to full-screen mode. See Chapter 7 for more on video chatting.

iChat menu bar icon

To change your status (whether you're available to chat or would prefer not to be bothered), you don't need to bring iChat to the front of all running applications. The iChat menu bar icon offers a shortcut for changing status, and also tells you which of your buddies is online and available (**Figure 1.5**). (Enable the menu bar icon in iChat's General preferences.) Selecting a buddy brings iChat to the front and initiates a text chat.

✔ Tips

■ Like nearly all windows in Mac OS X, you can minimize and zoom chat windows. Click the green Zoom button to expand the chat window, or click the yellow Minimize button to squeeze the chat window into the Dock. When a chat is minimized, it's still active: other people can send text messages, and the audio of audio and video chats continues (though you can't see the video feed) (**Figure 1.6**).

■ You can switch between iChat windows without using your mouse by pressing Command-~ (tilde).

■ When the iChat menu bar icon is active, you don't need the iChat application running to receive chats. In iChat's General preferences, disable the option labeled "When I quit iChat, set my status to Offline" to take advantage of this feature.

Getting Connected

When you use the telephone to call someone, your voice is not being carried down a single wire connected directly to the other person's phone. Instead, the signal goes out to a local switching box that routes your call through a number of different switches until it reaches your friend.

Instant messaging with iChat works much the same way over the AIM network, but it's also capable of connecting two or more iChat participants on a local network using Apple's Rendezvous technology.

AOL Instant Messaging (AIM)

When you start iChat, it connects to the AIM network, which directs chat traffic between all iChat and AIM clients connected to the Internet. While iChat is open, it's constantly checking in with the network to see if any of your buddies are online, their status, and if they're sending you messages. iChat also broadcasts the same information about you.

When you or a buddy initiates a chat, the AIM servers connect your clients so you can send messages back and forth. AIM also hosts group chat areas where more than two people can participate in a chat. (See Chapter 5 for details on the different types of text chats that are available.)

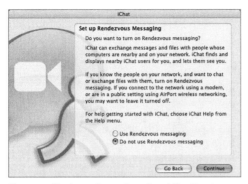

Figure 1.7 You have the option of enabling Rendezvous messaging the first time you launch iChat AV.

Figure 1.8 Use the status popup menu to sign in using Rendezvous.

Figure 1.9 iChat's two buddy lists.

Rendezvous messaging

You don't need to be connected to AIM to use iChat—in fact, you don't even need Internet access if all you want to do is chat with friends or coworkers on a local network. iChat supports Rendezvous (`www.apple.com/macosx/features/rendezvous/`), Apple's open-source networking technology that easily connects Rendezvous-enabled devices (like Macs, printers, and even things like TiVo personal video recorders) that are on the same network.

When you launch iChat for the first time, you're given the option of enabling Rendezvous messaging in one of the welcome screens (**Figure 1.7**). However, you can also turn it on and off manually.

To enable Rendezvous messaging:

1. Open iChat's preferences and click the Accounts icon.

2. Click the checkbox labeled "Enable local Rendezvous messaging" to turn it on or off. A separate Rendezvous window appears.

3. Close the preferences window.

To log in using Rendezvous:

◆ Choose Log In to Rendezvous from the iChat menu, or press Command-Option-L.

◆ Click the status popup menu beneath your name, and choose an Available or Away status message (**Figure 1.8**).

After logging in to Rendezvous, you'll see any other users on the network who also have Rendezvous messaging enabled (**Figure 1.9**).

CREATING YOUR iCHAT PERSONA

Online chatting has gotten a bad reputation as something used by 40-year-old men pretending to be 18-year-old co-eds (or vice versa). Undoubtedly, the idea of using a pseudonym or alternate identity appeals to some people, and you can certainly use iChat to be whomever you want. This is especially common in public chat rooms, where lots of people sign in to discuss topics of interest such as movies or computers.

But iChat's strengths lie in connecting people who already know one another: family members, friends, co-workers, and project collaborators, to name a few.

In iChat, you're also more than just a screen name. In addition to having a personalized image (see Chapter 3, *Your Buddy Icon*), you can express yourself with the font and colors used for outgoing text messages, or by the status message that other people see next to your name in their Buddy Lists.

Obtaining a Screen Name

To use iChat, you must have either an Apple .Mac (pronounced *dot Mac*) account or an AOL Instant Messenger (also known as AIM) account. Both services allow you to sign up for free screen names.

.Mac

Apple's .Mac is a subscription service that offers remote file storage, shared iCal calendars, online photo albums, and special software discounts and giveaways, as well as an iChat screen name. It also costs $100 per year. If you already subscribe to .Mac, use your mac.com email address (such as `ichatvqs@mac.com`) as your iChat identity.

However, if you aren't currently a .Mac subscriber, and don't particularly want to shell out the $100, you're in luck. As of this writing, Apple is offering a free 60-day trial subscription to .Mac; if you decide not to pay for the full service, you still get to keep your .Mac address to use with iChat. Go to Apple's Web site (`www.mac.com/1/ichat.html`) to sign up.

AIM

If you already have an AOL account, your screen name is also used as your iChat identity. If not, and you'd prefer to use an AOL screen name, go to the AIM Web site (`www.aim.com`) to sign up for a free account.

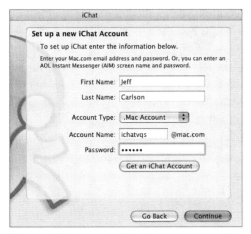

Figure 2.1 You're prompted to set up a new account when you first launch iChat.

Figure 2.2 No video camera? Don't worry—you can set one up later (I think Apple just wants you to know how cool iChat AV is).

Creating Your Persona

When you start it for the first time, iChat prompts you to create an identity. This is where you enter the bare-bones information. (To configure a persona without going through the following setup screens, see "Switching to Another Account," later in this chapter.)

To create your persona:

1. Launch iChat. An introductory screen appears. Click Continue.

2. Enter your first and last names in the fields provided (**Figure 2.1**).

3. From the Account Type popup menu, choose .Mac Account or AIM, depending on the type of service you have. For .Mac accounts, you only need to enter the first part of your email address, not "@mac.com".

   If you don't yet have an account, click the Get an iChat Account button, which launches a Web browser and takes you to Apple's .Mac site.

4. Enter your account name and password in the appropriate fields, and click Continue.

5. If you expect to use iChat primarily on your local network, enable Rendezvous messaging in the next window. (See Chapter 1 for more information about Rendezvous.) Click Continue.

6. Lastly, iChat checks to see if you have a video camera connected to your Mac to use for video chats (**Figure 2.2**). Click Continue (I'll cover video in more depth in Chapter 7).

7. Click Done on the last screen to exit the setup process. The Buddy List window appears and iChat logs into the AIM network.

Setting Your Status

Anyone who has added you to their Buddy List can see when you're logged in. Some people might take that as an invitation to chat (which is the whole point of instant messaging), but sometimes you need to keep your head down and get work done without interruption. In that case, you can switch your status from Available (green) to Away (red), while still being able to send messages to other people and not going offline entirely.

iChat's status indicator is one way of staying connected behind a sign that says "Keep Out."

To change your status:

1. The status message below your name is a popup menu in disguise—click it to view the status options (**Figure 2.3**).

   or

   Click the iChat menu bar icon to display its menu.

2. Choose either Available or Away.

A third indicator, Idle (yellow), is triggered when you haven't interacted with your computer for 10 minutes or more (Apple's iChat help claims 15 minutes, but I've seen Idle appear after as little as 6 minutes). If you set your status to Away, choose how iChat should note your availability when you return.

To automatically set status when returning to your Mac:

1. Open iChat's preferences, and click the General icon if it's not already selected.

2. Under the heading, "When I return to my computer, and my status is Away", choose an action and click its radio button (**Figure 2.4**). If you choose "Ask what to do," a dialog box appears when you return to your Mac (**Figure 2.5**).

3. Close the preferences window.

Figure 2.3 Click the status message popup window to set your status as Available or Away.

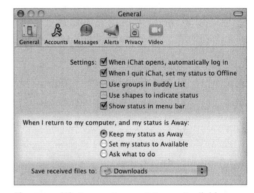

Figure 2.4 iChat can set your status as Available or leave it as Away when you return to your Mac.

Figure 2.5 You can also opt to decide your availability each time you come back to your computer.

SETTING YOUR STATUS

Figure 2.6 Use shapes to the left of each name, instead of colors, to indicate availability of people in your Buddy List.

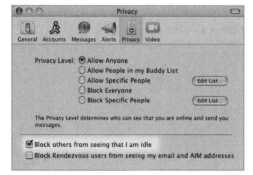

Figure 2.7 Enabling this setting broadcasts your status as Available or Away, even when you're Idle.

To change the appearance of the status indicators:

1. Open iChat's preferences and select the General icon.

2. Enable the option labeled "Use shapes to indicate status." Instead of seeing colored sphere icons beside each person's name (difficult for those who are color blind), you'll see colored shapes: a green circle for Available, a red square for Away, and an orange triangle for Idle (**Figure 2.6**).

3. Close the preferences window.

✔ Tips

■ Even if you've set your status to Away, other people can still send you messages and invite you to chats. If you really don't want to be interrupted, set your status to Offline. (Also see Chapter 5 for how to decline a chat invitation, and Chapter 4 for information on blocking other users.)

■ You may not want other people to see your status as idle: your boss might think you're not working, or you might be concerned that someone will know you're not around and try to steal sensitive information from your office or computer (unfortunately, it happens). If this is the case, go to iChat's preferences, click the Privacy icon, and enable the option labeled "Block others from seeing that I am idle" (**Figure 2.7**).

■ Have you missed a meeting? Check your colleagues' statuses in iChat. I can often tell when the editors of *Macworld* magazine are in a meeting because their iChat status indicators are idle and ticking away for about the same amount of time.

SETTING YOUR STATUS

13

Customizing the Status Message

I'm rarely either hot or cold. Usually my body temperature is somewhere in-between, depending on the weather, on whether I'm active or sedate (or even on if I'm feeling out of sorts). Similarly, I'm often not just "Available" or "Away" in iChat—sometimes I'm open to a friendly chat as long as the other person knows in advance that I can't spend much time at it. It's also a good way to let people know you're away but will be back soon ("Getting Coffee" tends to appear often on my machine). This is why it's possible to customize the status message that appears in other people's Buddy Lists.

There are two ways to change the message text: on the fly, which is quick, or via a dialog that also enables you to easily create multiple messages.

To customize the status message on the fly:

1. Click the status message popup menu and choose the Custom option belonging to either the Available or Away items.

2. Type your new message in the field that appears (**Figure 2.8**).

3. Hit Return or click outside the field to apply the change. The new message now appears in the popup menu (**Figure 2.9**) and the iChat menu bar menu.

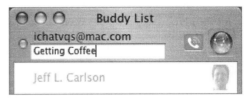

Figure 2.8 Choose Custom from the popup menu and then type in a custom status message.

Figure 2.9 Custom messages appear in the popup menu after you create them.

Figure 2.10 Use the status message dialog to create several custom messages at once.

To customize the status message via the dialog:

1. Choose Edit Status Menu from the status message popup menu.

2. Click one of the plus-sign (+) buttons to add a message (**Figure 2.10**).

3. Type your message and press Return. When you're finished editing, click OK. All of the entries appear when you click the status message popup menu or the iChat menu bar icon.

To remove a custom status message:

1. Choose Edit Status Menu from the status message popup menu.

2. Select a message entry.

3. Click the minus-sign (–) button to remove the message.

To re-order status messages:

1. Choose Edit Status Menu from the status message popup menu.

2. Drag a status message to another location in the list. Click OK when you're done.

✔ Tips

■ Drag the bottom-right corner of the Edit Status Menu dialog to resize it.

■ By default, the on-the-fly custom messages are stored with any that you create using the Edit Status Menu dialog. If you'd rather they exist as one-off messages instead, deselect the Remember custom messages checkbox in the dialog.

■ A few utilities exist to customize the status line in creative ways. iChatStatus, for example, displays the artist and title of the song that's currently playing in iTunes. See Appendix B for more utilities and add-ons.

CUSTOMIZING THE STATUS MESSAGE

Changing Your Text Appearance

The text messages you send appear in 12 point Helvetica type by default, but I find Helvetica to be difficult to read; I prefer a good serif font for reading chunks of text. You can change the font, size, and style, as well as your text balloon colors. The font and color options also apply to how your text will display to other iChat users. (See Chapter 5 to learn how to override others' appearance settings.)

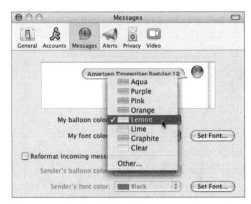

Figure 2.11 iChat includes eight preset balloon colors, which work well behind black text.

To change the color of balloons and text:

1. Open iChat's preferences, and click the Messages icon.

2. Click the My balloon color popup menu or the My font color popup menu to view a list of preset colors (**Figure 2.11**). (The color controls are the same for both items.)

3. If you want to use a custom color, choose Other in the popup menu.

4. In the Colors dialog, choose the color you'd like to use (**Figure 2.12**). The sample preview in the Messages window updates to reflect your selection.

5. Close the dialog when you're done.

Figure 2.12 Choose a color using the Mac OS Colors dialog.

To change the font:

1. Open iChat's preferences, and click the Messages icon.

2. Click the Set Font button. The Font dialog appears (**Figure 2.13**).

3. Choose a font family, typeface, and size.

4. Close the Font dialog when you're done.

Figure 2.13 The preview text in the preferences window displays text in the typeface that you choose in the Font dialog.

✔ Tips

■ When you're text chatting, you can display messages as either balloons or as colored blocks of text (see Chapter 5). This option is available once you've started a text chat, but in iChat's preferences you can preview how each style will appear. With the Messages preferences active, go to the View menu to display the sample preview as text or balloons.

■ Remember that other iChat users see the typeface that you specify... including the font size. Yes, it's possible to shout your words in 72 point bold text, but it's not nice to the folks using iChat in a small message window. (But sometimes it's just too satisfying to crank up the text, as well.)

CHANGING YOUR TEXT APPEARANCE

Setting the Chat Background

Apple could have easily kept the background color of text chat windows stark white, the default. But, of course, they didn't leave it at that. You can change the background color of any text chat window, or use an image (parchment paper, perhaps?).

To start a chat (without first sending a message), select a buddy's name in the Buddy List and click the Text Chat button. (I know, I'm getting ahead of myself a bit here. Jump to Chapter 5 briefly to learn how to start or receive a text chat.)

To set the chat background:

◆ Drag an image file from the Finder to the chat window (**Figure 2.14**). Be sure you drop the file on the window's background to avoid sending the file to the other chat participant.

   or

1. Choose Set Chat Background from the View menu.

2. Select an image file in the dialog that appears (**Figure 2.15**) and click Open. The image appears in the background for all new chats (**Figure 2.16**).

To clear the chat background:

With the chat window active, choose Clear Background from the View menu.

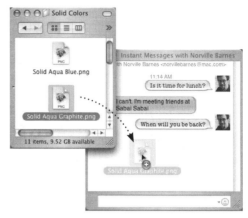

Figure 2.14 Drag an image file from the Finder to a chat window to change the background.

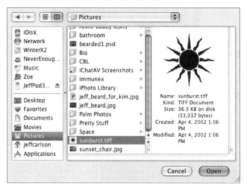

Figure 2.15 Another option is to select an image file using a standard Open dialog box.

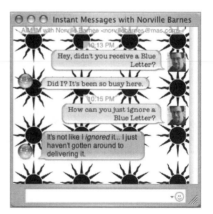

Figure 2.16 Today's lesson is: what *not* to use for a chat window background.

Figure 2.17 Choose Clear Background from the View menu to avoid unexpected drag-and-drop mistakes.

✔ Tips

■ To make a background image appear in all of your chat windows, use the menu option method above instead of drag-and-drop.

■ The background appears only on your Mac, not in other participants' chat windows.

■ You can't scale a background image, which means that most photos you take with a digital camera will have only a small portion visible in your chat window. Smaller images with repeating textures work well.

■ If you'd prefer a solid color background, you need to use an image containing that color. You don't have to look far: Apple includes some Desktop patterns in [Your Computer]/Library/Desktop Pictures/ Solid Colors/.

■ Sometimes when I'm sending an image file to someone (see Chapter 8), I miss the message field and drop the file onto the chat background (**Figure 2.17**). If this happens, choose Clear Background from the View menu.

Configuring Alerts

Most of the time, iChat works in the background, checking on your buddies and waiting for incoming chats. To get your attention and make it easy to identify what's happening, iChat uses a series of audible and visible alerts.

To configure alerts:

1. Open iChat's preferences, and click the Alerts icon.

2. Choose an event from the Event popup menu (**Figure 2.18**).

3. Choose an alert action by selecting one or more action checkboxes:

   ▲ **Play sound.** Apple includes a number of sounds that are tailored to specific iChat events. You can also choose any system alert sound, which appears in the Play sound popup menu (**Figure 2.19**). Some events, such as Text Invitation, can be set to replay the sound until you take action; click the Repeat checkbox to activate this feature.

   ▲ **Bounce icon in the Dock.** For a visual alert, enable this option by clicking its checkbox. The iChat icon bounces once; click the Repeat checkbox to make the icon bounce multiple times until you make iChat active.

   ▲ **Speak text.** For a more direct option, enable the Speak text option and write a message for your Mac to speak. Use the atmark (@) symbol to indicate the name of a user (such as telling you which user has initiated a chat). The Speech volume slider at the bottom of the screen controls how loud the voice plays.

4. Close the preferences window to apply the changes you made.

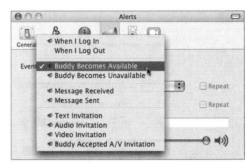

Figure 2.18 Alerts with sounds enabled appear with a speaker icon to the left of the event name.

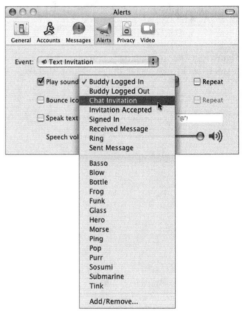

Figure 2.19 Apple's iChat sounds appear at the top of the Play sound popup menu. The standard system sounds appear below.

Figure 2.20 Add your own sounds, or those that other people have created (I downloaded these from www.pixelhaus.com).

Figure 2.21 Instead of using iChat's dialog, simply copy sound files using the Finder.

To add or remove other sounds in iChat:

1. From the Play sound popup menu (see previous task), choose Add/Remove.

2. In the dialog that appears, click the Add button, which lets you locate a sound file on your hard disk (**Figure 2.20**).

   To remove a sound, select it and click the Remove button.

3. Click Done when finished.

✔ Tips

- If you don't like your Mac bleeping and clicking and whirring at you, uncheck the Play sound options for each event.

- Change the speaking voice in Mac OS X's Speech preference pane.

- In addition to iChat's interface for adding other alert sounds, you can use the Finder to copy audio files to your Sounds folder at [User name]/Library/Sounds (**Figure 2.21**). You need to quit iChat and relaunch it for the sounds to appear in the Play sound popup menu.

CONFIGURING ALERTS

Switching to Another Account

If you have multiple .Mac or AIM accounts, you can switch between them in iChat without much difficulty.

To add another account:

1. Open iChat's preferences and click the Accounts icon.

2. Type your screen name into the AIM Screen Name field (**Figure 2.22**).

3. In the AOL Instant Messenger Login dialog that appears, enter your password (**Figure 2.23**). To bypass this screen in the future, enable the option labeled Remember password in keychain.

4. Click the Log In button.

To switch between accounts:

1. Open iChat's preferences and click the Accounts icon.

2. Click the popup menu next to the AIM Screen Name field to view a list of other identities you've used (**Figure 2.24**).

3. Choose another identity from the list. Or, choose Use my .Mac account to use the name and password stored in Mac OS X's .Mac preference pane (in Mac OS X 10.3 Panther) or the Internet preference pane (in Mac OS X 10.2 Jaguar).

4. Enter your password, if necessary.

Figure 2.22 If you have a separate .Mac or AIM account name, type it into this field.

Figure 2.23 Enter the password for the new account you will be using.

Figure 2.24 If you've used multiple accounts, their names appear in the popup menu.

Figure 2.25 Use the iChat menu (or press Command-L to log in and out of AIM).

Logging In and Out

Normally, iChat logs into the AIM network at startup, and logs out when the application quits. You can change this behavior using a few options in iChat's preferences.

To manually log in and out of AIM:

◆ From the iChat menu, choose Log In to AIM or Log Out of AIM, depending on whether you're currently logged in (**Figure 2.25**).

◆ If you're logged in, choose Offline from either the status message popup menu or the iChat menu bar menu.

If you're logged out, choose an Available or Away message from either menu to log back in.

To control when to log in:

1. Open iChat's preferences and click the General icon.

2. Enable or disable the option labeled "When iChat opens, automatically log in" to set iChat's initial behavior.

3. Enable or disable the option labeled "When I quit iChat, set my status to Offline." When disabled, you can still receive messages even when iChat isn't running (though iChat launches when a message comes in).

You can select available buddies and initiate chats if the iChat menu bar is active; doing so launches the iChat application.

Setting Your Privacy Level

How can I put this delicately? Sometimes it's necessary to control which people can send you messages. iChat's Privacy Level makes it easy to politely rebuff individuals.

To set your Privacy Level:

1. Open iChat's preferences and click the Privacy icon (**Figure 2.26**).

2. Choose one of the following options by clicking its Privacy Level radio button:

   ▲ **Allow Anyone:** Anyone who has added you to their Buddy List can see when you're online and send you messages.

   ▲ **Allow People in my Buddy List:** Only the people in your list can send messages.

   ▲ **Allow Specific People:** This option builds a list of people who can send messages. Unlike the previous option, you don't need to maintain a long Buddy List comprised of people you may not correspond with often. Click the Edit List button to add screen names.

   ▲ **Block Everyone:** When you really want to be left alone, but don't want to admit it by signing out of the AIM network completely.

   ▲ **Block Specific People:** This option creates a list of screen names; your name shows up as inactive (gray) in these people's Buddy Lists, preventing them from sending you messages. (For more on blocking people, see Chapter 4.)

3. Close the preferences window.

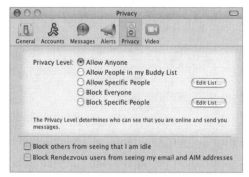

Figure 2.26 The Privacy Level setting determines who can send you messages.

Your
Buddy Icon

Perhaps I shouldn't make assumptions at this point. Maybe you're perfectly happy to exist on the Internet as a generic blue sphere (if you signed up with .Mac) or a little yellow running guy (for AIM users). It could be a fluke that you're using a Macintosh, a computer that embodies the notions of creativity and self-expression. And it's entirely possible that you prefer text-only, command-line interfaces devoid of all these curvy windows and drop shadows.

But I doubt it.

Although I know a few people for whom the last description is appropriate, one of the first things new iChat users ask about is their buddy icon, the small picture that is displayed in others' Buddy Lists and while chatting. The buddy icon is more than just a head shot—most of my buddies use logos, artwork, or other images as buddy icons, and switch between them depending on their moods. iChat is a tool for communicating, and your buddy icon can communicate a lot without even opening up a chat window.

iChat supports two methods of changing your buddy icon: importing an image file, or taking a video capture directly within iChat.

Importing Images

A buddy icon is simply a small image, which means you can use any photo or illustration as long as it's in a format that QuickTime understands. You don't even need to prepare the file in advance—even if you have a large image (for example, a group of people), you can crop it so that you only see one person's face. (However, there are some advantages to touching up images before bringing them into iChat, as I describe later in this chapter.)

To import an image file:

◆ Drag an image file from the Finder onto your buddy icon (**Figure 3.1**).

or

1. Choose Change My Picture from the Buddies menu, or click the buddy icon next to your name and choose Edit Picture from the popup menu. The Buddy Picture dialog appears.

2. Click the Choose button to locate an image file on your hard disk and click the Open button. The image appears full size in the image preview area (**Figure 3.2**).

To crop an image:

1. Drag the horizontal zoom slider to focus on a specific area of the image. The edges of the selection box indicate where the image will be cropped (**Figure 3.3**).

2. Click anywhere on the image and drag to reposition it within the selection box (**Figure 3.4**).

To use the image as your buddy icon:

Click the Set button to make the image your buddy icon. Or, click Cancel to discard your settings and start again.

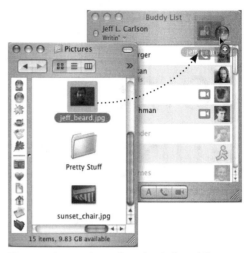

Figure 3.1 Drag an image from the Finder to iChat to use it as your buddy icon.

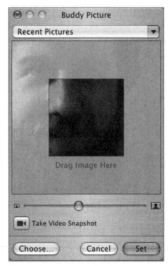

Figure 3.2 Imported images appear full size in the Buddy Picture dialog.

IMPORTING IMAGES

Zoom slider

Figure 3.3 Use the zoom slider to resize the image.

Reposition image within active area.

Figure 3.4 Click and drag the image to reposition it.

✔ Tips

■ Looking for pictures to use? If you use iPhoto to organize your digital photos, you can drag pictures directly from iPhoto to your buddy icon to open the Buddy Picture dialog.

■ That old Macintosh standby, Copy and Paste, also works for importing pictures, saving you the hassle of exporting image files. Simply copy an image in your favorite image-editing application (or word processor, or email client, or whatever will let you copy an image), open the Buddy Picture dialog using the steps on the previous page, and choose Paste from the Edit menu (or press Command-V). Heck, you can even copy a range of text and turn it into your buddy icon, though it will probably be unreadable.

■ If you need still more sources for buddy icons, head to the Web. A Google search for "aim buddy icons" produces numerous Web sites offering free downloads.

Taking a Video Capture

If you own an iSight or DV camcorder, you can take a snapshot of yourself within iChat that becomes your buddy icon.

To take a video capture:

1. Ensure that an iSight or DV camcorder is connected to your Mac (see Chapter 7 for details on setting up a camera).

2. Choose Change My Picture from the Buddies menu, or click the buddy icon next to your name and choose Edit Picture from the popup menu (**Figure 3.5**).

3. In the Buddy Picture dialog, click the Take Video Snapshot button. You'll have a few seconds to preen in the video feed that appears, while a red dot blinks to indicate the countdown before the image is taken (**Figure 3.6**). After about six seconds, the image is captured, complete with a simulated flashbulb effect.

To use the image as your buddy icon:

If the image looks good, click the Set button to make it your buddy icon (**Figure 3.7**). Or, click the Take Video Snapshot button again to grab a new image.

✔ Tips

- Were you too far away from the camera? See the next section for instructions on how to crop the image before setting it as your buddy image.

- For something different, try iChat Streaming Icon (ichat.twosailors.com), which takes multiple pictures to approximate a buddy icon video feed. It can consume a fair bit of your buddies' processing power as their machines frequently load new icon images (which might be annoying enough that they won't want to be your buddy anymore, so use with care).

Figure 3.5 Choose Edit Picture from the buddy icon popup menu.

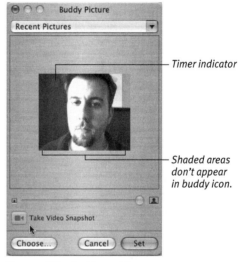

Timer indicator

Shaded areas don't appear in buddy icon.

Figure 3.6 The flashing red timer indicator tells you when a picture is about to be taken.

Figure 3.7 The captured image (left) is resized and turned into your buddy icon (right, with enlargement).

Figure 3.8 iChat's zoom feature doesn't always get in close enough, turning you into an amorphous blob.

Resized by iChat   *64 x 64 pixels*   *32 x 32 pixels*

Figure 3.9 Resizing the buddy icon in an image editor tends to improve its appearance, compared to iChat's default resizing capabilities.

Crop the image in an image editor such as iPhoto or Photoshop.

Resize the image to 32 by 32 pixels

Sharpen the image.

Figure 3.10 Improve the appearance of your buddy icon by (clockwise from left) cropping the image, resizing it to match iChat's measurements, and sharpening to bring out details.

Making Better Buddy Icons

Apple has made it easy to add just about any image to iChat by performing the calculations required to shrink an image to a 32 by 32 pixel icon. However, the reduction process often makes images blurry, or sometimes doesn't zoom as close as you'd like.

Using an image editor such as Graphic-Converter (www.lemkesoft.de), Adobe Photoshop (www.adobe.com/photoshop/), or iPhoto, you can perform some easy edits to improve the appearance of your icons.

To make better buddy icons:

◆ **Zoom in.** In iChat or an image editor, crop the photo tight around a person's face to show the most features. This also ensures you don't hit a zoom limit when using a larger photo (**Figure 3.8**).

◆ **Resize to fit.** iChat uses two icon sizes: 64 by 64 pixels for the icon that appears in the Address Book application and iChat's Get Info windows (see Chapter 4), and 32 by 32 pixels for the icon in iChat's Buddy List. Rather than leave the resizing up to iChat, do the work yourself in an image editor so you know what you'll end up with (**Figure 3.9**). Note that if you import a 32 by 32 pixel version, you'll need to use the zoom slider to zoom in on the icon to avoid seeing extra white space that appears.

◆ **Sharpen.** Resizing an image tends to blur its details. After resizing your picture in an image editor, use its sharpening tools to bring back some details (**Figure 3.10**).

✔ Tip

■ Even if your source image is at a higher resolution, you need to save your icons at 72 dots per inch (dpi), or iChat will resample it for you.

Using Multiple Buddy Icons

iChat keeps track of the last 14 buddy icons you used to make it easy to switch between them. Depending on your mood, you can project a bright cheery smile, put on your "angry eyes," or even display the logo of your current favorite sports team, if you want.

To switch to another buddy icon:

1. Click your buddy icon to reveal a grid of recent pictures (**Figure 3.11**).

2. Click the image you want to use.

To clear recent pictures:

1. Click your buddy icon.

2. Choose Clear Recent Pictures from the menu. You will be asked if you want to continue (**Figure 3.12**).

3. Click OK to clear the icons, or Cancel to return to the Buddy List.

✔ Tips

■ When you add a buddy picture, it appears at the upper-left corner position, while the other images shift one space to the right or down to the next row. When you have more than 14 icons, older ones drop off—but the generic .Mac globe and your Mac OS X user remain in place. To ensure that an image isn't deleted, choose it as your icon, which moves it to the upper-left slot.

■ When you clear recent pictures, two images remain in the list: the generic .Mac globe and the image associated with your Mac OS X user.

Figure 3.11 Choose a recent picture by clicking on the buddy icon and selecting one from the list.

Figure 3.12 If you continue, you lose all of your recent icons (but if they're as dorky as all the shots of me that appear in this book, it's probably not a bad thing).

THE BUDDY LIST

At first glance, the Buddy List appears to be just a list of names and pictures, a mundane collection of addresses waiting to be clicked—an email address book, but with pictures.

But then you see the list move: buddies' names show up in bold or fade to gray, addresses shift up and down depending on availability, icons and status messages change. The Buddy List is an up-to-the-second record of who's online at any given time.

In addition to determining how the Buddy List appears, you can use it to work with buddies in groups, view and set extra information for each buddy, and specify actions and alerts keyed to buddy activities.

Adding Buddies

It's fine to talk to yourself every once in a while, but eventually you'll need to strike up a conversation with someone else, or risk getting sideways glances from people passing by. It's worse in iChat, where chatting with yourself is more commonly known as "word processing." Fortunately, there are a few ways to add buddies to your Buddy List.

To add a new buddy (who is not in your Address Book):

1. If you know someone's screen name, click the plus-sign (+) button at the bottom-left corner of the Buddy List, choose Add a Buddy from the Buddies menu, or press Command-Shift-A. A dialog displays your Address Book information (**Figure 4.1**).

2. Click the New Person button.

3. In the next dialog, choose either .Mac or AIM from the Account Type popup menu, and enter your buddy's screen name in the Account Name field (**Figure 4.2**).

4. Enter the person's first and last names in the fields provided; although these fields are optional, leaving them blank will display only the screen name in your Buddy List, which can be confusing if the person's identity is actually "joe12345678" or something equally unidentifiable.

   Also optional is the Email field (see Chapter 8). If you have an icon you'd like to use for this person, drag the image file to the Buddy Icon field; however, I recommend leaving it blank for now, since your buddy will likely have his own icon.

5. Click the Add button. Your buddy now shows up in the Buddy List. If the person is online, their name appears in black text; if offline, their name and icon are grayed out (**Figure 4.3**).

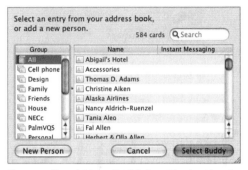

Figure 4.1 Your Address Book information is at hand when adding a new buddy to your Buddy List.

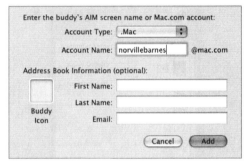

Figure 4.2 Choose an account type and enter your buddy's screen name here.

Figure 4.3 Offline buddies appear in gray. Once the person signs in, the name shows up black.

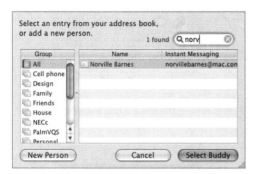

Figure 4.4 If a buddy already exists in your Address Book, find his name by typing in the search field.

Figure 4.5 When someone initiates a chat, but you don't have them in your Buddy List, use the Buddies menu to add them.

To add a buddy from your Address Book:

1. Click the plus-sign (+) icon, choose Add a Buddy from the Buddies menu, or press Command-Shift-A.

2. Find your friend's name by typing it in the search field or scrolling to it (**Figure 4.4**).

3. Click the Select Buddy button.

   If you don't have a .Mac or AIM account name in that person's Address Book entry, a dialog appears where you can enter the screen name (see Step 3 on the previous page).

To add a buddy from an incoming chat:

When someone initiates a chat with you, but doesn't appear in your Buddy List, choose Add Buddy from the Buddies menu, or press Command-Shift-A. The menu includes the person's screen name (**Figure 4.5**).

If he exists in your Address Book, he shows up in the Buddy List. If not, you're given the option to enter his name and email using the same dialog from the previous task.

To edit a buddy's address information:

1. Select a person in the Buddy List.

2. Choose Get Info from the Buddies menu, or press Command-Shift-I. A dialog appears showing the person's address card.

3. Edit the name, email, and instant messaging (AIM) information in the fields provided.

4. Click OK to close the dialog.

ADDING BUDDIES

To remove a buddy from the Buddy List:

1. Select a buddy in the Buddy List; the buddy can be active or inactive.

2. Press the Delete key, or choose Delete from the Edit menu. A confirmation dialog appears (**Figure 4.6**).

3. Click OK to delete, or Cancel to return to the Buddy List.

✔ Tips

■ You can also add a person to your Buddy List from the Address Book application. In the Card and Columns view, drag a contact from the Name column directly into the Buddy List; in Card Only view, click and hold on the title bar icon for a second, then drag to the Buddy List (**Figure 4.7**).

■ Where's your buddy's icon? Often when you add someone to your Buddy List, their icon doesn't show up right away. Wait a few minutes for the network to pass along the information. Restarting iChat usually refreshes the buddy icons; asking your buddy to change her icon can sometimes force the image to update.

■ Don't feel obliged to add every incoming person to your Buddy List. Occasionally I receive a chat from someone who was given my screen name from a friend, and who has a short question or two.

■ Adding someone to your Buddy List is something that happens only on your computer—you're not automatically added to the other person's list, and they aren't notified that you've added them.

Figure 4.6 A confirmation dialog asks if you really want to remove the buddy. The person's entry is not removed from your Address Book, however.

Figure 4.7 Drag contacts from the Address Book application directly to your Buddy List.

- Removing people from the Buddy List does not delete them from Address Book.

- If you switch computers or use a different AIM-compatible chat application, your Buddy List remains intact. The information is stored on an instant messaging server, and is retrieved when you log into the network.

- Use the keyboard to select buddies. Hit Tab to select your buddy icon, then hit Tab again to highlight the list—you'll see a faint blue glow around the list. Then use the arrow keys to select a buddy.

ICQ, MSN, and Yahoo

iChat's use of the AIM network potentially connects you to millions of people, but AIM isn't the only flavor of chat out there. To connect to someone's ICQ ("I Seek You") account, enter their ICQ number in the AIM field when adding the buddy.

Unfortunately, iChat does not currently work with Microsoft's MSN network or Yahoo's chat network, but separate chat clients are available as free downloads for the Mac: MSN Messenger for Mac (`messenger.msn.com/Mac/`) and Yahoo Messenger for Mac (`messenger.yahoo.com/messenger/download/mac.html`).

ADDING BUDDIES

iChat and Address Book

iChat uses the Address Book database to store your buddy information. As a result, the two programs tie into each other in convenient ways.

For example, when a buddy is online and his status is Available, a green indicator appears in his Address Book entry (**Figure 4.8**). You can also initiate chats from Address Book. In iChat, the information from the Address Book enables you to send an email message using your preferred email software, and store a custom buddy icon.

You can also assign multiple screen names to one person. A friend of mine, who alternates between a handful of different screen names, appeared multiple times in my Buddy List. Then I got wise and added all of his identities to his entry in my Address Book. Now he shows up once in my Buddy List, no matter how many screen names he uses.

To view a buddy in Address Book:

1. Select a name in your Buddy List.

2. Choose Show in Address Book from the Buddies menu. Address Book opens and displays the person's information.

To initiate a chat from Address Book:

1. Locate the person with whom you wish to chat in Address Book. If they're online, a green sphere icon appears to the left of their name.

2. Click the green icon. Or, click the label for the AIM field and choose iChat from the popup menu that appears (**Figure 4.9**). A dialog appears, asking you which type of chat you'd like to initiate (**Figure 4.10**).

3. Click the Text Chat, Audio Chat, or Video Chat button to start the chat.

Online indicator

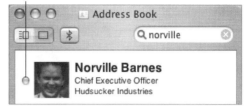

Figure 4.8 You can see who's online by browsing your Address Book records.

Figure 4.9 Click the instant messaging field label and choose iChat from the popup menu to start a chat.

Figure 4.10 After clicking the green online indicator, choose which type of chat you want to initiate.

ICHAT AND ADDRESS BOOK

Figure 4.11 Click the plus-sign icon to add more AIM screen names.

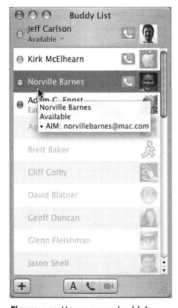

Figure 4.12 Hover over a buddy's name to see his screen name.

To send an email message from within iChat:

1. Select a name in your Buddy List.

2. Choose Send Email from the Buddies menu, or press Command-Option-E. A new, pre-addressed outgoing email is created in your preferred email software. (For more on sending email and working with the Mail application, see Chapter 8.)

To store multiple screen names for one person:

1. In Address Book, locate the person's card you wish to edit.

2. Click the Edit button, choose Edit Card from the Edit menu, or press Command-L.

3. Click the plus sign (+) button to the left of the instant messaging field and type the screen name (**Figure 4.11**).

4. Click the Edit button again to switch out of editing mode.

✔ Tip

■ Hold your mouse pointer over an entry to view that buddy's screen name (**Figure 4.12**). This information appears only when the buddy is online.

Customizing the Buddy List Display

Entries in your Buddy List appear with the person's name or screen name, a buddy icon, an audio or video status icon, and a status message if the person has entered a custom one. You can customize this display to minimize the amount of screen real estate the Buddy List occupies (**Figure 4.13**).

It's also possible to change how your buddies are sorted in the list.

To customize the Buddy List display:

Select the following options from the View menu to enable or disable them:

◆ **Show Buddy Pictures.** This toggles the display of buddy icons. Turning this option off saves you a lot of room if you want to keep the Buddy List window as small as possible (**Figure 4.14**).

◆ **Show Audio Status.** When disabled, the green audio status icon is hidden.

◆ **Show Video Status.** If you disable this option, you won't see the video status icon. However, this icon only appears if you have a video camera connected to your computer (and if your buddy also has a video camera connected to his computer).

◆ **Show Offline Buddies.** Normally, offline buddies appear grayed out in the Buddy List. Turning off this option hides them entirely (**Figure 4.15**).

Figure 4.13 A greatly minimized Buddy List.

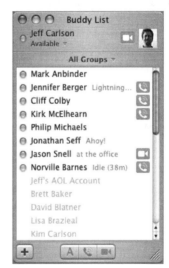

Figure 4.14 The Buddy List takes up less space when buddy icons are hidden.

Figure 4.15 For a cleaner appearance, hide offline buddies.

Figure 4.16 Sorted by first name.

Figure 4.17 Sorted by last name.

To sort the Buddy List:

Choose one of the following options from the View menu; only one can be active at a time:

◆ **Sort by Availability.** Buddies who are available are moved to the top of the list, and further sorted according to their status: Available, Idle, or Away. The entries are also sub-sorted by last name; for example, in my Buddy List, when Norville Barnes becomes available, his name appears above Cliff Colby's name. But if Norville switches his status to Away, his name is kicked down below the group of Available buddies. This is iChat's default behavior.

◆ **Sort by First Name.** Entries are sorted by first name, regardless of which buddies are available (**Figure 4.16**).

◆ **Sort by Last Name.** Entries are sorted by last name, again regardless of availability (**Figure 4.17**).

✔ Tip

■ If you prefer to sort by first or last name, but want to keep all available buddies visible, turn off the Show Offline Buddies option in the View menu.

Viewing More Buddy Information

iChat can display a little more information about each buddy than what you enter when you add someone to your list. Earlier in the chapter, you learned how to edit the address information by way of the Info dialog; in this section, I'll describe what else you can do there, such as specifying a buddy image and adding personal notes.

The Info dialog also contains a field that displays an AIM profile, a short section of text that allows other instant messaging users to find out a bit more about you.

To view more buddy information:

1. Select a person in your Buddy List.

2. Choose Get Info from the Buddies menu, or press Command-Shift-I. The Info dialog appears (**Figure 4.18**).

To change a buddy's icon:

1. In the Info dialog, choose Address Card from the Show popup menu.

2. Drag an image file from the Finder to the Picture field. Or, copy an image from another application, click the Picture field to select it, and paste the image.

3. To use your picture instead of the one your buddy chose, select the box marked "Always use this picture." This feature is useful if you'd prefer that the icons in your Buddy List don't change, and is visible only on your machine.

✔ Tip

■ You can only get information about a buddy who appears in your main (AIM) buddy list. The Get Info command is unavailable for buddies that appear in the Rendezvous buddy list.

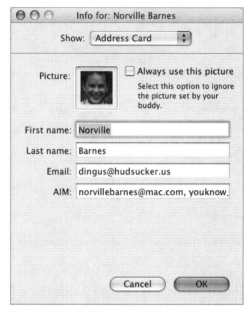

Figure 4.18 The initial screen in the Info dialog is the Address Card, which gets its information from Address Book.

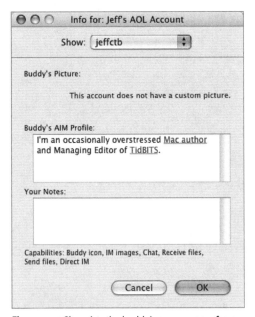

Figure 4.19 Choosing the buddy's screen name from the Show popup menu gives you a user-created profile and an area to write notes.

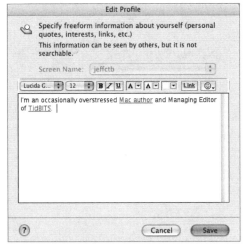

Figure 4.20 iChat offers no way to enter a profile for yourself, so you need to fire up the AOL Instant Messenger application to create one.

To add notes about a buddy:

1. In the Info dialog, choose your buddy's screen name from the Show popup menu.

2. Type text into the Your Notes field (**Figure 4.19**). This information is visible only to you, not to your buddy.

3. Click OK.

To add profile information using AOL Instant Messenger:

1. iChat doesn't offer a way to input profile information, but you can do it in the AOL Instant Messenger application. Download and install the software from *www.aim.com*.

2. Choose Edit Profile from the AIM menu.

3. Enter any personal information you want to share in the text field (**Figure 4.20**). You can use different fonts, styles, and add links to Web sites.

4. Click Save when you're finished.

5. Choose Quit from the AIM menu to exit the program. Now, anyone who looks at your information in iChat (or AIM) will see the profile you entered.

VIEWING MORE BUDDY INFORMATION

Setting Buddy Actions

In Chapter 2, I explained how you could configure alerts in iChat's preferences, which let you assign an action—playing a sound, for example—to various events such as when a buddy becomes available. You can configure the same sort of actions for each buddy, as well, allowing you to identify a specific buddy and action when iChat is in the background. Think of this feature as the chatting equivalent to custom ringtones on your cellular phone.

To assign buddy-specific actions:

1. In the Info dialog, choose Actions from the Show popup menu (**Figure 4.21**).

2. Choose an event to customize from the Event popup menu.

3. Depending on the event, choose one or more of the following actions by selecting their checkboxes.

   ▲ **Play sound.** Choose a sound from the popup menu. Select the Repeat checkbox to make the sound repeat until you switch to iChat; some events, such as Buddy Becomes Available, don't support repeated sounds (if they did, you'd go insane). When you apply a sound to an event, a small speaker icon appears to the left of the event name in the popup menu (**Figure 4.22**).

   ▲ **Bounce icon in the Dock.** This option is handy when your Mac's volume is muted, or when you plug in a pair of headphones but forget to put them on (speaking from experience…). As with sounds, you can choose to make the action repeatable, but only for certain events.

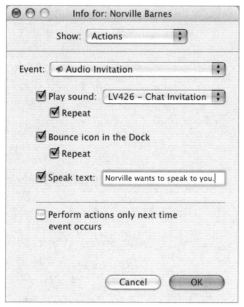

Figure 4.21 Set up custom actions for individual buddies based on iChat events.

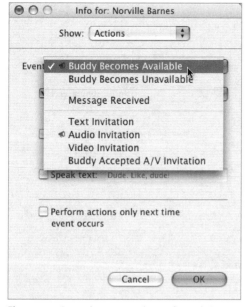

Figure 4.22 Several events can be configured. A speaker icon appears if a sound is specified.

▲ **Speak text.** Using the Mac's built-in speech synthesis, iChat can relay any text you type into this field. Instead of assigning lots of random sounds for multiple buddies, I prefer that a voice simply says something like, "Brett has arrived" or "Toby has left the building...good night!"

▲ **Perform actions only next time event occurs.** If you're expecting a chat and want an action to happen once, select this option. As soon as the event happens, the event is reset.

SETTING BUDDY ACTIONS

Managing Buddy Groups

It's a sad, but, alas, inevitable occurrence. At some point we become too popular, resulting in a Buddy List so long that it's almost impossible to keep track of everyone. How to cope with the attention, the demands, the outpouring of so much good will? It vexes me, truly.

Fortunately, iChat provides some assistance. You can set up groups of buddies to help organize your Buddy List. This is handy when you want to set up a group chat, but don't want to cherry-pick the people from your full list.

To start using buddy groups:

1. Open iChat's preferences, and click the General icon.

2. Select the "Use groups in Buddy List" checkbox (**Figure 4.23**), then close the preferences window.

To create a new group:

1. Choose Show Groups from the View menu, or press Command-Shift-G. The Groups drawer appears to the left of the Buddy List.

2. Click the plus-sign (+) icon at the lower-left corner of the Groups drawer. A new unnamed group appears (**Figure 4.24**).

3. Type a name and press Return.

✔ Tip

- If you later decide not to use groups, go to iChat's preferences, click the General icon, and deselect "Use groups in Buddy List." This removes the Groups popup menu above the list (but the groups you set up still exist).

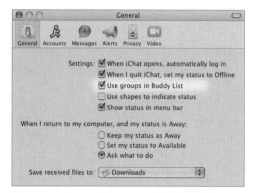

Figure 4.23 Turn on "Use groups in Buddy List" to start assembling buddies into groups.

Figure 4.24 Click the plus-sign button on the Groups drawer to create a new buddy group.

Figure 4.25 If a buddy belongs to only one group, removing the person deletes him from the Buddy List.

Figure 4.26 Be sure to hold down Option when dragging a buddy to a group to ensure that he doesn't get deleted from the Buddy List accidentally.

Adding a Buddy to a Group

It should be as easy as dragging a buddy's name from the Buddy List to a group name. Unfortunately, it's actually not so simple. By default, every buddy is automatically added to the "Buddies" group. However, contrary to the behavior of established Apple programs such as iTunes and iPhoto, when you drag a buddy to another group, the buddy is removed from the "Buddies" group. This creates problems when you want to remove a buddy from that group: iChat assumes that if a buddy belongs to just one group, removing it from the group means deleting the buddy entirely (**Figure 4.25**)!

To add a buddy to a group:

Option-drag a buddy's name from the Buddy List to a group name. This *copies*, not moves, the buddy to that group. A green plus-sign (+) icon appears on your mouse pointer to indicate that a copy is being made (**Figure 4.26**).

To remove a buddy from a group:

1. Be sure the buddy also appears in the "Buddies" group (see above).

2. Select the buddy you wish to remove.

3. Press the Delete key, or choose Delete from the Edit menu.

   If the buddy does not also belong to the "Buddies" group, iChat asks if you want to delete them from the Buddy List. Click Cancel unless you really want to delete them entirely.

To remove a group:

1. Be sure that any buddies in the group also appear in the "Buddies" group (see previous page).

2. Select the group name in the Groups drawer.

3. Press the Delete key, or choose Delete from the Edit menu.

If any buddies in the group do not also belong to the "Buddies" group, iChat asks if you want to delete those buddies from the Buddy List (**Figure 4.27**). Click Cancel, unless you really want to delete them.

To view groups:

◆ Choose a group name from the Groups popup menu above the Buddy List (**Figure 4.28**).

or

1. Choose Show Groups from the View menu, or press Command-Shift-G, to display the Groups drawer.

2. Deselect the All Groups checkbox.

3. Select the checkbox for one or more of the groups listed in the drawer. The Buddy List updates to reflect your choice.

✔ Tips

■ To close the drawer quickly, click the right-facing arrow button at the top. To resize it, drag the left edge of the drawer.

■ There is a Buddy List limit: according to Apple, you can have 150 buddies before strange things happen, such as buddies disappearing from the list and statuses not being reported. (Some people have reported having 190 or more buddies.)

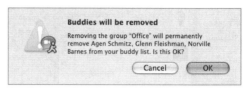

Figure 4.27 When multiple buddies are part of just one group, deleting the group removes them from the Buddy List.

Figure 4.28 The Groups popup menu is a quick method of displaying buddies from specific groups.

MANAGING BUDDY GROUPS

5

TEXT CHAT

It all starts with the written word. Long before microphone inputs or digital cameras were commonplace, people communicated across the Internet using plain, old-fashioned text. And although audio and video get the splashy attention (see the next two chapters), most people use iChat to communicate via text.

The brilliant thing about iChat is that text isn't relegated to an afterthought: the designers at Apple worked hard to make text messages easy to read (you'd be surprised at how difficult a normal conversation can be in some other chat programs). And it's more functional than the pretty facade would indicate, letting you control who sends you messages, manage group chats with several participants, and customize the look and feel of each conversation.

Initiating a Text Chat

iChat offers three types of text messages: *instant* and *direct* messages, which involve just two participants, and *group chats* where three or more people are involved. (See "Text Chat in Groups," later in this chapter, for more on group chats.)

In most cases, you initiate an instant message to someone else: the text you type is sent to an AIM network server, which relays it to the person you're chatting with. In the case of a direct message, a connection is created between your Mac and your buddy's computer, without AIM acting as middleman. Direct messages are slightly more secure than instant messages, but aren't always supported; for example, a buddy connecting from behind a corporate firewall may not be able to receive direct messages.

To send an instant message:

1. Select a person in your Buddy List.

2. Click the Text Chat button at the bottom of the Buddy List window. You can also choose Send Instant Message from the Buddies menu, press Command-Option-M, or choose Send Instant Message from the contextual menu (Control-click the buddy's name, **Figure 5.1**).

3. In the blank message window that appears, start typing in the text field; a thought-cloud icon appears to indicate that you're typing (**Figure 5.2**). At this point, a connection hasn't been opened, so the other person does not know you're about to chat.

4. Press Return or Enter to send the message. When your buddy replies, his text appears in the message window (**Figure 5.3**).

Text Chat button

Figure 5.1 The contextual menu is just one method of initiating a text chat; clicking the Text Chat button is also convenient.

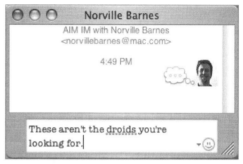

Figure 5.2 Start typing to begin a text chat; the other person is invited after you send your first message.

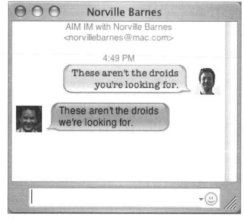

Figure 5.3 Your buddy's text appears below yours in a new message balloon.

Figure 5.4 iChat indicates that the session is a Direct Message session.

Figure 5.5 If someone isn't in your Buddy List, you can still invite them to chat.

To send a direct message:

1. Select a person in your Buddy List.

2. Choose Send Direct Message from the Buddies menu, press Command-Shift-Option-M, or choose Send Direct Message from the contextual menu.

3. Enter some text and press Return or Enter. iChat indicates in gray after your message that a direct instant message session has started (**Figure 5.4**).

To initiate a new chat with someone who is not in your Buddy List:

1. Choose New Chat with Person from the File menu, or press Command-Shift-N. A new message window appears with a drop down dialog.

2. Enter the person's screen name in the field marked "Enter the address of the person to invite" (**Figure 5.5**), and click OK.

3. Type into the text field and press Return or Enter to start the chat. (See Chapter 4 for instructions on how to add this person to your Buddy List.)

✔ Tips

- iChat lists the type of text chat at the top of the message window in gray text. It also periodically notes the time that messages have come in.

- When you're chatting with someone using Rendezvous messaging, the Direct Message option is not enabled. However, because Rendezvous works only on a local network, you're actually chatting using direct messages, even if iChat doesn't label them as such.

INITIATING A TEXT CHAT

To correspond via text:

Simply type text and press Return or Enter to send it. When the other person is typing, a thought-cloud icon appears until they send the message (**Figure 5.6**).

To exit a chat:

Close the message window.

However, closing the window only terminates the chat on your end. If the other person replies in their message window, a new window appears on your screen, and does not include any text from your previous conversation.

✔ Tips

- When you're performing a text chat over Rendezvous, the letters you write are sent to the other person in bursts as you type (**Figure 5.7**). Personally, I'm not a fan of this feature, because not only is it distracting, the other person sees your thoughts as you compose them. For those of us who type, delete, then retype again, it's an annoyance. To turn this feature off, open iChat's preferences, click the Messages icon, and deselect "Send text as I type (Rendezvous only)".

- Press Option-Return to enter a line break without sending the message.

- Use key commands when typing messages to navigate your text (**Table 5.1**).

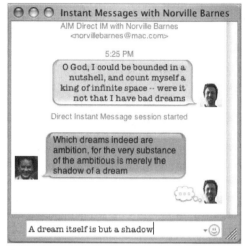

Figure 5.6 A thought-cloud icon appears to alert the other person that you're typing a message.

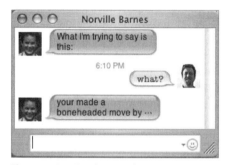

Figure 5.7 In a Rendezvous chat, you can see what the other person is typing as they type it.

Table 5.1

Keyboard Shortcuts for Editing Text	
SHORTCUT	ACTION
Esc	Erase the text field
Control-A	Go to start of line
Control-E	Go to end of line
Control-D	Erase forward
Control-O	Open another line
Control-P	Go up a line
Control-N	Go down a line
Option-Delete	Delete a word

Incoming chats   iChat icon in Dock

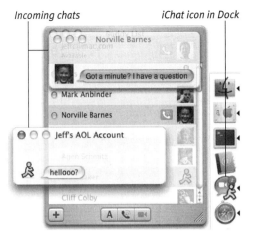

Figure 5.8 Each incoming chat appears in its own window; the iChat icon in the Dock tells you how many chats are pending.

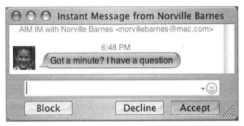

Figure 5.9 Choose which action to take when a chat request arrives.

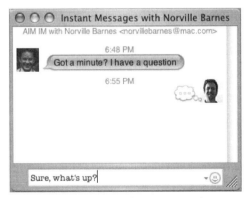

Figure 5.10 Click the Accept button to open the incoming chat, and type your reply.

Receiving a Text Chat

When someone else wants to chat with you, a window appears in iChat containing the person's text. Depending on how you set your alerts preferences (see Chapters 2 and 4), a sound plays and iChat's icon bounces in the Dock; the icon also displays a number to indicate how many chat requests are pending (**Figure 5.8**).

To receive a text chat:

When an incoming chat invite appears, click the window to make it active, which displays the following buttons (**Figure 5.9**):

◆ **Accept.** Click this button, or type a reply into the text field and press Return or Enter (**Figure 5.10**).

◆ **Decline.** To decline the invitation, click this button or close the window.

◆ **Block.** This button enables you to block certain people from seeing that you're available. See "Blocking a Person," on the next page.

Blocking a Person

Occasionally, you may want to prevent someone from initiating a chat with you: perhaps the person chats too frequently, or someone is hassling you electronically, or you just need to work for a while without being interrupted by casual chats. You can log out of iChat, of course, but that prevents you from chatting entirely.

When you block someone, they see your name as being offline in their Buddy List—they don't know that you've intentionally blocked them. When they've come back into your good graces, you can unblock them in iChat's preferences.

To block a person:

◆ When an incoming chat arrives, click the Block button. A dialog asks if you're sure you want to block all future chats with that person; click Block (**Figure 5.11**).

   or

1. Open iChat's preferences and click the Privacy icon.

2. Select the Block Specific People radio button, and click the Edit List Button.

3. In the dialog that appears, click the plus-sign (+) button and type the screen name of the person to block (**Figure 5.12**).

4. When you're finished adding names, click Done.

Figure 5.11 Block a person to prevent them from ever chatting with you (until you turn off blocking, that is).

Figure 5.12 Add the screen names of people you wish to block in iChat's Privacy preferences.

To unblock a person:

1. Open iChat's preferences and click the Privacy icon.

2. Go to the Block Specific People option and click the Edit List button.

3. Select the name of the person you wish to unblock, and click the minus-sign (−) button.

4. Click Done.

✔ Tips

- To ensure that no one sends you an instant message, select Block Everyone in iChat's privacy preferences.

- Blocking works only for chatting over the AIM network; Rendezvous buddies can't be blocked.

Talking with Chat Bots for Fun and Information

People aren't the only ones chatting online. A number of "chat bots"—software that can answer questions using an instant messenger interface—offer information such as online games, news headlines, and more.

For example, choose New Chat with Person from the File menu (or press Command-Shift-N), type "ZolaOnAOL", and then type something such as "hi". Typing keywords delivers real-time information, such as "weather seattle wa" or "thesaurus procrastinate" (**Figure 5.13**).

Other handy chat bots include "AOLYellowPages", which looks up phone numbers and addresses, and "recipebuddie," which directs you to online recipes. Add the bots' screen names to your Buddy List if you find them useful. To find more, search at Google.com for "aim chat bots".

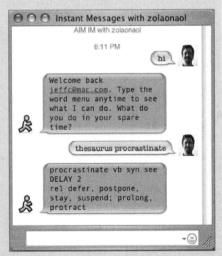

Figure 5.13 Chat bots such as ZolaOnAOL automatically retrieve information for you, such as this handy thesaurus.

Text Chat in Groups

As the Managing Editor of *TidBITS*, a weekly Macintosh newsletter (www.tidbits.com), I'm part of a truly virtual organization. Of the editors, three of us live in Washington State (separated by at least 30 minutes of driving, with good traffic), three live in New York, and one lives in California. Although we use email and the phone to communicate, often it's faster and easier to set up a group text chat in iChat to hash out an issue or coordinate tasks without the time-delayed nature of email or the awkwardness (or the costs) of a telephone conference call.

Group chats operate much like normal one-on-one text chats, but with a few group-specific variations, such as ignoring someone in a chat and adding new people.

To initiate a group chat:

1. Select two or more people in your Buddy List.

2. Choose Invite to Chat from the Buddies menu or the contextual menu, or click the text chat button at the bottom of the Buddy List; you can also simply press Return or Enter. A new message window opens, with the Participants drawer revealed (**Figure 5.14**).

3. Type an invitation message in the text field and hit Return. The participants receive a chat invitation and have the option of accepting or declining. If they accept, their text appears in the message window (**Figure 5.15**). As people enter the chat, each participant sees the list of who is involved in the chat.

Figure 5.14 The Participants drawer slides out to reveal the people invited to a group chat.

Figure 5.15 Everyone else in the chat appears on the left side of the message window.

TEXT CHAT IN GROUPS

Figure 5.16 Drag people from your Buddy List to the Participants drawer of an active group chat.

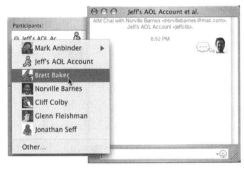

Figure 5.17 The plus-sign (+) icon at the bottom of the Participants drawer displays all online buddies.

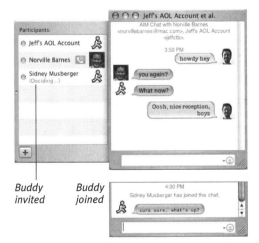

Buddy invited   Buddy joined

Figure 5.18 After you've extended an invitation, the person's status reads "Deciding" until they join.

To add more people to a group chat:

1. With a group chat in progress, drag a person (or several) from your Buddy List to the message window's Participants drawer (**Figure 5.16**).

   Or, click the plus-sign button at the bottom of the Participants drawer to display a popup menu of buddies who are currently online, then select a person's name (**Figure 5.17**).

2. Enter an invitation message, then click the Invite button. The buddy's status message indicates that they're deciding to join the chat (**Figure 5.18**). If they join, their text appears in the message window.

✔ Tips

- Your buddy icon and text balloon always appear on the right side of the message window; everyone else shows up on the left side.

- Group chats cannot be made over Rendezvous, nor can you mix AIM and Rendezvous participants.

- You need to add someone to your Buddy List before you can invite them to a group chat (see Chapter 4).

- Group participants do not see any discussion that's occurred before they arrived, so it's a good idea to wait until everyone is present before getting to the meat of your conversation.

- Any member of the group chat can invite other people using the steps above.

To show and hide chat participants:

◆ Choose Hide Chat Participants from the View menu to make the Participants drawer disappear.

◆ Drag the resizing handle, located on the left edge of the drawer, to the message window.

To ignore a person:

1. Select the name of the person to ignore in the Participants drawer.

2. Choose Ignore [buddy's name] from the Buddies menu. Any comments made by that person will not show up in your message window (**Figure 5.19**).

   To stop ignoring the person, choose the Ignore [buddy's name] menu item again.

Your chat window

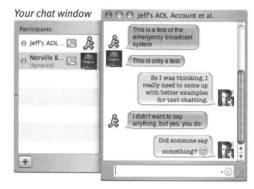

Ignored buddy's chat window

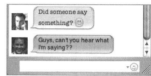

Figure 5.19 When you ignore a buddy, he can see the entire conversation, but you can't see his comments.

Text Chat Etiquette

Although text chatting occurs in real time, it's not the same as talking on the phone or in person. Here are some general rules and words of advice for when you're chatting with someone:

◆ As with email, don't write in ALL CAPS. It gives the impression that you're SHOUTING.

◆ iChat gives you the option of setting a default font and text size (see later in this chapter), but don't abuse it by setting your chat font to 24 point Arial Black. Other people see the font you choose, and though they can set their iChat preferences to format all incoming text, they shouldn't have to.

◆ If someone's status is set to Away, don't initiate a chat with them. I was (rightly) bawled out by a colleague for chatting while he was on a deadline once.

◆ It's often better to post in bursts of a sentence or two, rather than composing a long paragraph of text before sending it off.

◆ Because there's often a slight delay between posts, usually when someone is composing a response, it's not unusual to have a few different topic threads going on at the same time. Sometimes it helps to introduce a new subtopic in parentheses. Then again, you'll find that you pick up on multiple threads fairly easily once you're in the midst of them.

◆ Some people use instant message acronyms that serve as shorthand for phrases that take too long to write out. Examples include: LOL (laugh out loud), YMMV (your mileage may vary), BRB (be right back), IMO (in my opinion), and BTW (by the way). For a good list of acronyms, see AOL's Acronym Dictionary (www.aim.com/acronyms.adp?aolp=).

Figure 5.20 Enter the name of a chat to create a new group. You can choose any name you wish.

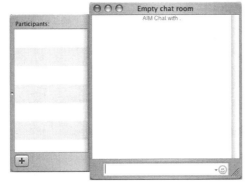

Figure 5.21 Your new, empty public chat room is open to anyone who knows the room's name.

Public Group Chats

When you create a group chat, it's given a name such as "jeffctb 123456789" so that AIM can track who is included. Because of this, you can create a group chat and host a virtual salon where anyone can show up for discussion. This option is good for pulling together a number of people who use iChat into one discussion without having to manually add each one—broadcast an email containing the date, time, and group chat name, and wait for everyone to show up.

Similarly, you can go to any group chat as long as you know the name of the chat. However, it appears that you cannot join in on AOL's popular community chat rooms using iChat; personally, I think this is a good thing, since many of them tend to be infested with automated chat bots that solicit adult Web sites.

To initiate a public group chat:

1. Choose Go to Chat from the File menu. The Go To Chat dialog appears.

2. Enter the name of your chat into the field provided and click Go (**Figure 5.20**).

   As long as you leave the message window open and remain connected to the AIM network, the chat room stays open (**Figure 5.21**).

To join a public chat:

1. Choose Go to Chat from the File menu (yes, you use the same command to create and to join public chats).

2. Enter the name of the chat room you wish to join, and click Go.

Checking Spelling

Judging from the informal chats between several of the people I know (who also happen to be writers and editors), you'd think that spelling and grammar had been outlawed. But that's the nature of impromptu chatting: writing perfect prose isn't as important as getting an idea across (in fact, those same writers and editors sometimes go out of their way to come up with the most egregious spelling and grammar errors).

Still, that doesn't give everyone license to abuse the language, so if you're concerned about spelling, use iChat's built-in spelling features.

To check spelling as you type:

Go to the Edit menu, select the Spelling submenu, and choose Check Spelling as You Type. iChat compares words to the spelling dictionary built into Mac OS X and marks possible misspellings with a red dotted underline as you compose your words (**Figure 5.22**).

To check spelling before you send:

1. Compose a message, but do not send it.

2. From the Spelling submenu of the Edit menu, choose Spelling, or press Command-: (colon). The Spelling dialog appears with any possibly misspelled words highlighted (**Figure 5.23**).

3. Choose one of the following options:

    ▲ If the Spelling dialog's choice of a replacement is the proper spelling, click Correct.

    ▲ If your spelling is correct, click Ignore.

    ▲ Click Find Next to bypass the current word and move onto another.

    ▲ If your word didn't appear in the dictionary, click Guess to prompt an alternative.

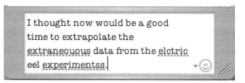

Figure 5.22 Spelling errors appear with a red underline to help you catch them. They want to be caught.

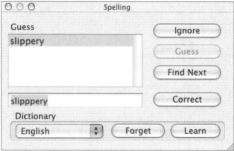

Figure 5.23 The Spelling dialog is a more incremental approach to correcting errors.

CHECKING SPELLING

▲ Click Learn to include your spelling in the current dictionary.

▲ Click Forget to remove a word from the dictionary.

4. Close the Spelling dialog.

✔ Tip

■ If the dotted red underlines of the Check Spelling as You Type feature annoy you, disable it and choose Check Spelling from the Spelling submenu, or press Command-; (semicolon) before you send the message. This option highlights words that it believes are misspelled, without using the Spelling dialog.

Inserting Smileys

One limitation of text communication is the lack of additional cues—such as voice tone or body language—to indicate the range of meanings that are easy to express over audio or video (or in person, even!). I could write, "You're going to pay for that," but by itself the phrase doesn't indicate if I'm joking or threatening.

As a shorthand for such situations, people developed *smileys* or *emoticons*, characters in text that reveal happiness, sadness, or various moods in-between. To view a text smiley, turn your head to the left and imagine a smiling face:

:-)

Instant message programs like iChat substitute graphical representations of smileys to make them more clear; **Table 5.2** contains the 16 smileys available in iChat.

To add a smiley:

◆ Type the characters that match the smiley. When you press the spacebar, the characters are automatically converted to their icon equivalent.

◆ Choose an icon from the smiley popup menu to the right of the text field (**Figure 5.24**).

◆ Choose an icon from the Insert Smiley submenu of the Edit menu.

✔ Tip

■ The Electronic Frontier Foundation hosts the "Unofficial Smiley Dictionary," with entries such as "User wears a toupee" ({:-)). Personally, my favorite smiley will always be Lyle Lovett (##:-|). (www.eff.org/Net_culture/Net_info/ EFF_Net_Guide/EEGTTI_HTML/ eeg_286.html)

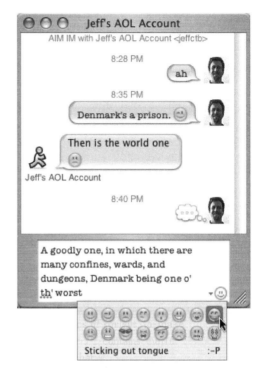

Figure 5.24 Smiley characters you type are automatically converted to smiley icons.

Table 5.2

iChat Smiley Icons		
CHARACTERS	MOOD	ICON
:-)	Smile	
;-)	Wink	
:-(	Frown	
:-/	Undecided	
=-o	Gasp	
:-D	Laugh	
:-*	Kiss	
:-P	Sticking out tongue	
:-[	Embarrassed	
:-!	Foot in mouth	
8-)	Cool	
>:-o	Angry	
0:-)	Innocent	
:'(	Cry	
:-X	Lips are sealed	
:-$	Money-mouth	

INSERTING SMILEYS

Figure 5.25 URLs are automatically recognized as hyperlinks when you type them into a message.

Figure 5.26 Highlight some text and apply a hyperlink so you don't clutter the message with a long URL.

Adding Hyperlinks

Frequently when I'm chatting, I want to point someone to a Web site containing more information about our conversation, or movie showtimes, or something funny that has to be seen. You can copy and paste URLs into the message field, and iChat recognizes them as Web addresses and makes them active links (**Figure 5.25**). But you can also add a hyperlink to selected text that your buddy can click on.

To add a hyperlink:

1. Type your message, and select a few words that will be hyperlinked.

2. Choose Add Hyperlink from the Edit menu, or press Command-K.

3. In the dialog that appears, type or paste a URL and click OK (**Figure 5.26**).

   If you've already added a hyperlink and want to get rid of it, click the Remove Link button.

✔ Tip

- If a word is hyperlinked in the message field, and you want to select it to edit the URL or remove the link, you can't just click it to position your cursor—clicking it opens the hyperlink. Instead, select a few letters before or after the word, bring up the hyperlink dialog, and click Remove Link to remove it.

Sending and Receiving Images

Don't be lulled by the black-and-white banality of text: iChat can sling multimedia files, too. You can send images directly to another person using the message window's text field.

To send an image:

1. Drag an image file from the Finder to the text field of the message window (**Figure 5.27**), or copy an image from another source and paste it into the text field.

2. Press Return or Enter to send the message. A smaller representation of the image appears as your message (**Figure 5.28**).

To receive an image:

If a buddy sends an image to you and you want to save the file, drag it from the message window to a location on your hard disk (such as the Desktop).

✔ Tips

- You can drag pictures from iPhoto's library to iChat's message text field without having to export the photo first.

- I've seen lags between the time that I send an image and when the recipient sees it, so if they're seeing nothing but a big gray box, wait a few minutes for the image data to transfer across the network.

- If you send an image to someone, an instant message switches to a direct message.

- Be sure to drag the image file onto the text field. If you drop it onto the message area, it could become the background for the message window (see Chapter 2).

Figure 5.27 Drag an image file from the Finder to the text field in the message window to send it.

Figure 5.28 iChat scales the image and displays it in a text balloon. Your buddy sees the same thing.

SENDING AND RECEIVING IMAGES

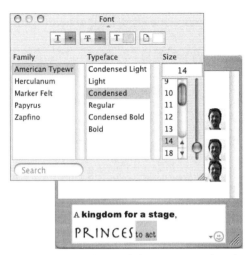

Figure 5.29 Using the Font dialog, you can apply multiple typefaces and sizes to a text message.

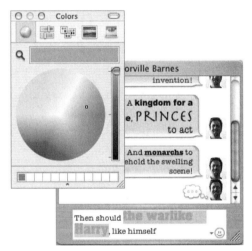

Figure 5.30 The full range of Mac OS X colors are available through the Colors dialog.

Changing Text Formatting

You can change the appearance of specific words and letters in the message window's text field.

To change font:

1. Highlight the text you wish to edit.

2. Choose Show Fonts from the Format menu, or press Command-T. The Font dialog appears.

3. Choose a family, typeface, and size for the text; iChat previews your selections in the message window (**Figure 5.29**).

4. Close the Font window when you're finished, or choose Hide Fonts from the Format menu.

To change the text formatting:

1. Highlight the text you wish to edit.

2. From the Format menu, choose Bold (Command-B), Italic (Command-I), or Underline (Command-U).

   You can also choose one of the formatting options prior to typing, then choose it again when you want to stop the effect.

To change color:

1. Highlight the text you wish to edit.

2. Choose Show Colors from the Format menu, or press Command-Shift-C. The Colors dialog appears.

3. Choose a color using one of the color pickers available (**Figure 5.30**).

4. Close the Colors window when you're finished, or choose Hide Colors from the Format menu.

✔ Tip

■ You can leave the Font and Colors dialogs visible while you use iChat.

Changing Message Appearance

iChat's use of buddy pictures and dialog balloons is certainly endearing, but it's not for everyone. If you prefer a less cartoonish appearance, a few options are available.

To set the message type:

Go to the View menu and choose Show as Text or Show as Balloons, depending on your visual preference (**Figure 5.31**).

To set buddy identification:

From the View menu, choose how buddies are identified in message windows: Show Names, Show Pictures, or Show Names and Pictures (**Figure 5.32**).

✔ Tip

■ The appearance options described here affect individual message windows; they don't set defaults for every new window.

Figure 5.31 If you think iChat's balloons look too much like a cartoon, set the message type to text.

Figure 5.32 Viewing only with pictures can make it difficult to identify who's speaking when people don't use custom buddy icons (top). Choose Show Names and Pictures to see labels with the icons (bottom).

Figure 5.33 Set all incoming messages to display the same font, size, and balloon color.

Figure 5.34 With a little work, your message window can resemble...Unix!

Reformatting Incoming Messages

Just as you can determine how your messages appear to others, you can also control how all incoming messages are formatted on your screen.

To reformat incoming messages:

1. Open iChat's preferences, and click the Messages icon (**Figure 5.33**).

2. Select the Reformat incoming messages checkbox.

3. Choose the message color from the Sender's balloon color popup menu; choosing Random picks a different color for each chat participant.

4. Use the Sender's font color popup menu and the Set Font button to specify the color and typeface for incoming text.

5. Close the preferences window when you're done.

✔ Tip

■ For a strictly bare-bones message window, choose Show as Text and Show Names from the View menu; set all incoming messages as one uniform font and size; and set the sender's balloon color as Clear (**Figure 5.34**).

Working with Chat Transcripts

Although it all starts with the written word, as I said at the beginning of this chapter, the word ends up being ephemeral and fleeting—once you close your chat window, the words disappear. If you'd rather keep your words around, save the transcripts of your chat sessions.

To save chat transcripts automatically:

1. Open iChat's preferences, and click the Messages icon.

2. Select the checkbox marked "Automatically save chat transcripts" (**Figure 5.35**).

   iChat saves the sessions as text files that contain special formatting so that when you open them later in iChat, you get the full visual formatting.

   The files' titles are the names of the people you chatted with, and can be found in the iChats folder within your Documents folder. Click the Open Folder button in iChat's preferences to automatically open that folder.

To save a chat transcript manually:

1. Choose Save a Copy As from the File menu, or press Command-S.

2. Choose a location on your hard disk, give the file a unique title, and click Save.

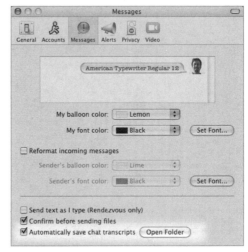

Figure 5.35 iChat can keep a record of every text chat for later reference when you enable this preference.

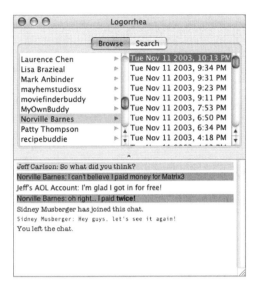

Figure 5.36 The freeware program Logorrhea browses and searches iChat transcripts sensibly.

To open a chat transcript:

Double-click the file in the Finder to open it in iChat. You can also choose Open or Open Recent from the File menu, and then locate the file.

✔ Tip

■ Frankly, it's insane to try to find a chat transcript by rooting around in the iChats folder. To work effectively with transcripts, check out Logorrhea (www.spiny.com/logorrhea/), an application that offers a sensible way of browsing chats plus a search feature for scanning the conversations (**Figure 5.36**). Logorrhea (which means "pathologically excessive talking") is freeware.

Audio Chat

We're all spoiled by the telephone. At the press of a few buttons, we can be talking to anyone with fairly good audio quality. It's like magic.

It turns out that accomplishing the same feat isn't as easy over the Internet. Because millions of data packets must cross dozens of servers just for a single connection, iChat AV needs to maintain sound quality and synchronization. Fortunately, iChat does all that work in a way that enables you to not only send bursts of speech or noise to another person, but to use your Mac as a speakerphone.

iChat uses full-duplex audio technology, which means you and a buddy can talk at the same time without being interrupted. And the audio codecs (a shorthand term for *compression/decompression*) used by iChat minimize feedback loops and deliver surprisingly clear voice quality.

That sounds impressive, but here's the real-world upside: iChat's audio capabilities enable you to use it to call other iChat users around the world—without paying long distance telephone rates. At the next holiday when the phone lines are jammed, you can talk to Grandma online whenever it's convenient.

Preparing for an Audio Chat

Audio chatting is built into iChat AV, but can your Mac setup take advantage of it? Here's a quick checklist of what you need to participate in an audio chat, plus information on setting an audio input source, depending on your model of Macintosh.

Requirements for an audio chat:

◆ **Microphone.** Depending on the model of your Macintosh, a microphone may be included. PowerBooks and iBooks (except for the earlier fruit-colored iBooks) all include either a built-in microphone or a line-in port for connecting one.

◆ **Internet connection.** To use iChat over the Internet, you need a connection speed of at least a 56K modem or better.

◆ **Speakers or headphones.** The better to hear you with, my dear. Even though your Mac includes a built-in speaker, the audio quality is better when played through external speakers or headphones (this is especially true for laptops; see the tip about laptops in the next section).

To set the audio input source:

1. Open iChat's preferences and click the Video icon.

2. Choose an input source from the Microphone popup menu (**Figure 6.1**).

✔ Tips

■ If you're using a video camera with a built-in microphone, iChat selects it automatically.

■ If your Mac doesn't include a microphone, consider purchasing Apple's iSight (which requires FireWire) or Griffin Technology's iMic USB audio input device (www.griffintechnology.com/products/imic/).

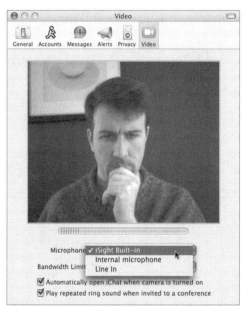

Figure 6.1 Go to the Video preferences to set the microphone source.

Figure 6.2 Buddies with an audio status icon can accept audio chats.

Figure 6.3 The Audio Chat button is active when you select a buddy who is capable of chatting via audio.

Figure 6.4 The Get Info dialog displays a buddy's chat capabilities, including Conferencing and Microphone.

Starting an Audio Chat

In order to participate in an audio chat, you need to make sure the other person's system and connection are capable, which is easy to figure out. Initiating an audio chat is similar to starting a text chat.

To determine if an audio chat is possible:

◆ Look in the Buddy List. If an audio icon appears to the left of your buddy's picture, you're good to go (**Figure 6.2**). (Be sure you've turned on Show Audio Status from the View menu, or this icon doesn't appear.)

◆ Select the buddy's name and look to see if the Audio Chat button is enabled, not grayed out (**Figure 6.3**).

◆ If you like to use the Mac's contextual menus, as I do, Control-click your buddy's name and see if Invite to Audio Chat is an option, and not grayed out.

◆ If you prefer to do things the long, hard way, select the buddy, choose Get Info from the Buddies menu, select the buddy's name from the Show popup menu, and look at the list of Capabilities at the bottom of the dialog. If you see "Conferencing" or "Microphone," you can participate in an audio chat (**Figure 6.4**).

✔ Tips

■ Do you have a microphone, but it's not picking up audio? iChat may not recognize it if you plugged in the microphone while the application was running. Quit iChat, unplug the microphone, plug it in again, and restart iChat.

■ If you don't have a microphone connected or enabled, you won't see audio status icons for any buddies.

STARTING AN AUDIO CHAT

To initiate an audio chat:

1. Select a person's name in the Buddy List.

2. Do one of the following:
   - ▲ Click the Audio Status button beside the buddy's icon.
   - ▲ Click the Audio Chat button at the bottom of the Buddy List.
   - ▲ Choose Invite to Audio Chat from the contextual menu.
   - ▲ Choose Invite to Audio Chat from the Buddies menu.

   An audio chat window appears with the message "Waiting for reply…" while the other person chooses to accept your invitation (**Figure 6.5**).

3. When the connection is made, start speaking. The sound level graph indicates how loud or faint the audio input is, helping you to know if you need to speak up or speak closer to the microphone (**Figure 6.6**).

   You can also use the volume slider to change the volume of your buddy's voice.

✔ Tips

- Audio chats operate one-on-one; you can't have multiple audio chats going on at the same time. If someone in your Buddy List is currently involved in an audio or video chat, their audio or video status icon appears dim (**Figure 6.7**).

- As I mentioned at the beginning of this chapter, audio chats are full-duplex, which means you and your buddy can speak at the same time without getting cut off (by the technology anyway; whether one of you tends to cut off the other in conversation is beyond the help I can offer).

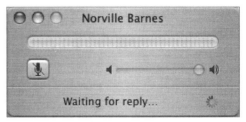

Figure 6.5 The Audio Chat window doesn't require much of an interface, as you can tell.

Sound level indicator   *Volume control slider*

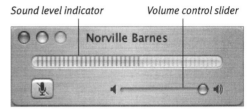

Figure 6.6 The sound level indicator registers how well the microphone is picking up audio signals.

Buddy is on another audio chat

Figure 6.7 When someone is already involved in an audio chat, the audio status icon is dimmed.

- You can minimize the audio chat window to the Dock and continue your conversation without interruption.

- To find out how long you've been chatting, open the Connection Doctor, which displays the call duration. See "Using the Connection Doctor," later in this chapter.

- Who stopped the music? If iTunes is running in the background, your music is automatically paused when an audio chat begins. When the chat ends, the music starts again where it left off.

- Does the audio coming out of the built-in speakers of your PowerBook G4 or iBook sound tinny or flat? This is by design: to reduce audio feedback from the internal microphone, the sound from audio and video chats comes out of the left speaker only, and in mono. Connect a set of headphones or speakers to improve the quality (though it's still mono). See Apple's support Web site for more information (`docs.info.apple.com/article.html? artnum=93214`).

STARTING AN AUDIO CHAT

Starting a One-Way Audio Chat

Don't you wish you had the last word sometimes? If you want to speak to someone, but they don't have a microphone (or they've disabled theirs), you can still initiate a one-way audio chat. This feature is good if you need to address a room full of people (similar to using a speakerphone) in a situation where they don't need to reply.

To initiate a one-way audio chat:

1. Select a person in the Buddy List.

2. Choose Invite to One-Way Audio Chat from the Buddies menu or from the contextual menu (**Figure 6.8**). An audio chat connection opens as described in the last task.

✔ Tip

■ If the other person has the capability to engage in an audio chat, the one-way audio chat option is disabled.

Figure 6.8 The contextual menu is often an easier launching point for a one-way audio chat.

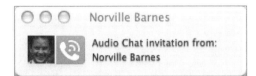

Figure 6.9 An audio chat invitation is clearly labeled as such. Click the dialog to activate it.

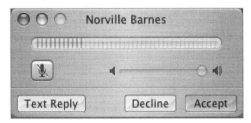

Figure 6.10 The Accept button is the default for an audio chat invitation, so you can hit Return to start.

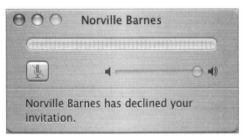

Figure 6.11 The status bar at the bottom of the window indicates if the other person declined to chat.

Figure 6.12 You can send a text message instead, allowing you to decline a chat invitation politely.

Receiving an Audio Chat

When someone initiates an audio chat with you, iChat rings and opens a new connection dialog (**Figure 6.9**). Choose one of the following options.

To receive an audio chat:

◆ Click the Accept button to open the audio connection (**Figure 6.10**).

◆ Click the Decline button if you don't want to participate. The other person is notified (**Figure 6.11**).

◆ Click the Text Reply button to decline the chat but send a message using a text chat (**Figure 6.12**).

✔ Tips

■ To configure the sound that iChat makes when an audio chat invitation comes in, or whether a sound is made at all, see Chapter 2.

■ To prevent others from inviting you to audio chats, choose Enable Microphone from the Audio menu (if a camera is attached to your Mac, the menu reads Video) to deselect it. When you want to initiate an audio chat with someone else, you'll need to re-enable this option.

Muting Audio

You can silence your outgoing audio without ending the audio chat, which is helpful when you need to talk with someone in the room with you, or if fire engines tend to scream past your office window (as they do past mine).

To mute audio:

◆ In an active audio chat window, click the mute button (**Figure 6.13**). Click it again to turn off muting.

◆ Press the spacebar. Press it again to stop muting.

✔ Tip

■ Is the quality of your audio degrading as you talk? Mute the connection, then un-mute it. iChat re-evaluates the bandwidth that's available and improves the connection.

Mute button

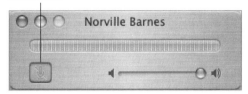

Figure 6.13 Mute an audio chat without disconnecting by clicking the Mute button or pressing the spacebar.

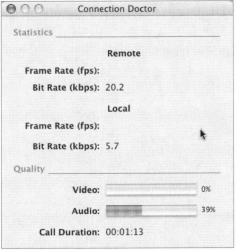

Figure 6.14 The Connection Doctor provides diagnostic information to help troubleshoot your connection.

Figure 6.15 This is an example of a not-so-great connection, between a Mac on a DSL connection and one connected by modem.

Using the Connection Doctor

The Connection Doctor provides some basic status indicators to help you diagnose problems with your audio or video connection. Choose Connection Doctor from the Audio menu (which appears as the Video menu, if a camera is attached to your Mac) to display the window (**Figure 6.14**). See Appendix A for some troubleshooting suggestions.

To use the Connection Doctor:

◆ The Statistics area displays the current bit rate in kilobits per second (kbps). (Frame rate is used in video connections, and appears blank for audio chats.) The Remote value is your buddy's connection; the Local value is yours.

  If one bit rate value is lower than the other, or is dropping rapidly, that could indicate a problem with the connection (**Figure 6.15**).

◆ The Quality area measures how much data is being lost in transit due to network congestion or line noise. (This is also referred to as *packet loss*, because it's a measurement of how many packets of data are being sent across the Internet.)

◆ The Call Duration displays the length of time the connection has been active, in hours, minutes, and seconds.

VIDEO CHAT

I've seen enough science fiction to know that the idea of holding a telephone handset up to my ear to communicate with someone is going to seem like such the quaint anachronism. Someday soon, I'll nod to a wall, say, "Call Nancy," and wait a few seconds while a videoconference session opens between us.

In the meantime, we have iChat AV. Provided you have the hardware and a broadband Internet connection, you can start video chatting with a friend in only a few clicks.

"But," you ask, "does anyone really *need* to chat via video? Do I want to comb my hair every time I want to talk to someone? Sure, it's a good showpiece during a Macworld Expo keynote, but *who's really going to use it*?"

Aside from the fact that being exceedingly cool is a reason in itself, I can already foresee some uses: grandparents who live far away can interact with their grandkids; company workgroups can collaborate visually in meetings that are more productive than using a speakerphone (just hook a Mac to a projector); school kids can have virtual in-class visits from people who can't make it in person (wouldn't it be cool if your Show and Tell item was a video chat with a NASA astronaut?).

I don't expect that video chatting will replace phones or email, but when you need that visual experience, iChat AV is ready.

Preparing for a Video Chat

Because you're dealing with a larger stream of data, the technical requirements for a video chat are steeper than for audio or text chats. Even with today's advanced compression algorithms, video is a lot of information to push down the pipe.

Requirements for a video chat:

◆ **A modern Macintosh.** Your Mac needs to have a PowerPC G3, G4, or G5 processor running at 600 MHz or faster.

◆ **A FireWire video camera.** Apple would love to sell you its $150 iSight (www.apple.com/isight/), which fortunately is a great compact video camera (**Figure 7.1**). It includes a built-in microphone, an auto-focus lens, and even a little green light to indicate when you're "on air." Best of all, to me, it's incredibly compact and stylish; I frequently carry mine in the same bag as my PowerBook.

However, you don't need an iSight. Other FireWire webcams include Unibrain's Fire-i (www.unibrain.com), Orange Micro's iBOT (www.orangemicro.com/ibot.html), or ADS Tech's Pyro 1394 Web Cam (www.adstech.com).

You can also use a DV camcorder as your video and audio source. Just plug it in via FireWire, and iChat recognizes it. If you thought you'd never use your camcorder again once you returned from vacation, now's the time. Even older non-DV camcorders can work if you have an analog-to-digital bridge device connecting it to your Mac.

Figure 7.1 Apple's iSight is well designed, compact, and features a microphone and auto-focusing lens.

Using a USB Webcam?

Although not officially supported, you can use some USB webcams, thanks to Ecamm Network's $10 iChatUSBCam (www.ecamm.com/mac/ichatusbcam/). In fact, according to the developers, it enables you to use iChat videoconferencing on machines that fall below Apple's recommended guidelines.

Figure 7.2 The video status icon indicates that a video camera is connected and recognized by iChat.

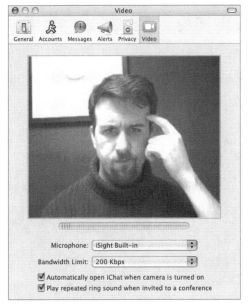

Figure 7.3 iChat's Video preferences show you what the camera is seeing.

◆ **Broadband Internet access.** To keep up with the flow of data, your Internet connection needs to be at least 100 kilobytes per second (Kbps), such as a cable or DSL connection. Unfortunately, satellite Internet access, which offers those types of speeds, has a spotty track record with video chatting due to high latency: it takes a relatively long time for a signal to travel from your computer to a satellite and back to another computer on the Internet, which disrupts the quality of the video feed.

To connect a video camera:

Plug the camera into your Mac. If it's recognized, the video status icon appears next to your picture in the Buddy List (**Figure 7.2**).

If no icon appears, check the Video menu to see if Camera Enabled is checked (if not, choose it to enable the camera). If that doesn't work, quit iChat, reconnect the camera, and launch iChat again.

You can also go to iChat's preferences and click the Video icon; you should see what the camera is seeing in the main preview area (**Figure 7.3**).

✔ Tips

■ If your DV camcorder is shutting itself off after a few minutes, remove the tape.

■ Avoid running multiple applications that would use your video camera, such as iMovie or Final Cut Pro. This isn't an issue with Apple's iSight, but it is with camcorders.

■ iChat's video preferences include an option marked, "Automatically open iChat when camera is turned on." Enable it to, well, automatically open iChat when a camera is turned on.

Previewing Your Video Image

One of the first things you'll want to do, after plugging in the camera, is make sure the camera is working and pointed at you correctly.

To preview your video image:

1. Click the video status icon next to your buddy icon in the Buddy List. This brings up a preview window (**Figure 7.4**).

2. Adjust the placement of your camera so that you're visible in the preview window. The audio level indicator also shows you how well the microphone is working.

✔ Tips

- You can also preview the video image in iChat's video preferences.

- Does something seem strangely amiss? iChat's preview is actually flipped, so that you see a mirror image of yourself, versus what the camera actually sees (**Figure 7.5**). Your buddy gets a true image, but the image of yourself is mirrored so you don't get disoriented.

- Most video cameras appreciate a good deal of ambient light. For a less muddied image of yourself, turn on a few more lights than normal. Or, if you can stand it, turn on those overhead fluorescent lights that you've been ignoring. (Can you tell I have a bias against fluorescent lighting? Unfortunately, they provide good lighting for video chatting.)

- If you have more than one video camera connected to your Mac, choose the camera you want to use in iChat's Video preferences.

Figure 7.4 Clicking the video status icon in the Buddy List brings up a preview window. And yes, you can use your camera as an expensive mirror. Bring up the video preview and preen away.

Figure 7.5 iChat displays your video preview flipped, as if you were looking in a mirror. On your buddy's screen, however, the image is not reversed.

Figure 7.6 If a video status icon appears next to a buddy's picture, it means you can chat using video.

Figure 7.7 The Video Chat button is active (not grayed out) when you select a buddy who can do video chat.

Figure 7.8 Since my iSight sits in the middle of the top of my PowerBook's screen, I place video chat windows as close to the camera as I can.

Starting a Video Chat

Initiating a video chat is as simple as starting a text or audio chat. First, check to make sure the other person can accept a video chat, then start it up. If you run into a snag, see Appendix A for some troubleshooting advice.

To determine if a video chat is possible:

◆ Look in the Buddy List to see if the video status icon appears next to your buddy's name (**Figure 7.6**). (Be sure that Show Video Status is enabled under the View menu.)

◆ Select a buddy and look to see if the Video Chat button is enabled, not grayed out (**Figure 7.7**).

◆ Control-click your buddy's name and see if Invite to Video Chat is enabled in the contextual menu.

◆ You can also select your buddy, choose Get Info from the Buddies menu, select their name from the Show popup menu, and look at the list of Capabilities at the bottom of the dialog. If you see "Camera," you can participate in a video chat.

✔ Tip

■ Position your chat window onscreen as close to your camera as possible; for example, on my PowerBook I put the window in the top-middle portion of the screen. This gives you closer eye contact with the other person while you're looking at them on your screen (**Figure 7.8**).

To initiate a video chat:

1. Select a person's name in the Buddy List.

2. Do one of the following:
   - ▲ Click the Video Status icon next to the buddy's picture.
   - ▲ Click the Video Chat button at the bottom of the Buddy List.
   - ▲ Choose Invite to Video Chat from the contextual menu.
   - ▲ Choose Invite to Video Chat from the Buddies menu.

   A video chat window opens while the other person chooses to accept your invitation (**Figure 7.9**).

3. When the connection is made, the preview image of you shrinks to occupy one corner of the window, and your buddy's video feed appears in the main viewer (**Figure 7.10**). Start interacting.

To end a video chat:

- ◆ Click the window's close button in the title bar, or choose Close from the File menu (or press Command-W).

- ◆ If you're in Full Screen mode, click the End Chat button, marked with an X, located in the controls that appear above the preview image (see later in this chapter for information on working in Full Screen mode).

✔ Tip

- ■ The video codecs that iChat uses are optimized for video without much movement (such as a talking head). To minimize the amount of image artifacts that appear, don't move around excessively (**Figure 7.11**).

Figure 7.9 When someone invites you to a video chat, you start by seeing a preview of your image while the other person decides whether or not to chat.

Figure 7.10 The preview of you shrinks down to one corner and the video feed of your buddy occupies most of the window once a video chat is started.

Figure 7.11 Excessive or fast motion tends to produce blurry or jagged video (and a headache).

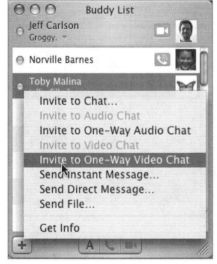

Figure 7.12 Start a one-way video chat using the contextual menu in your Buddy List.

Starting a One-Way Video Chat

If your buddy doesn't have a video camera, but does have a qualifying Mac, you can initiate a one-way video chat. They see and hear you, and you can hear their audio. This is the feature to use for transmitting your Big Brother messages (but watch out for flying hammers).

To initiate a one-way video chat:

1. Select a person in your Buddy List.

2. Choose Invite to One-Way Video Chat from the Buddies menu or from the contextual menu (**Figure 7.12**). A video chat window opens.

✔ Tips

- If both participants have cameras attached, the one-way video chat option is disabled.

- The one unnerving thing about one-way video chats is that you're looking only at yourself in the video window. I prefer to minimize the chat window to get it out of the way (click the yellow minimize button on the window's title bar, choose Minimize from the Window menu, or press Command-M). That way I can concentrate on looking at the camera.

- Does the audio coming out of the built-in speakers of your PowerBook G4 or iBook sound tinny or flat? This is by design: to reduce audio feedback from the internal microphone, the sound from audio and video chats comes out of the left speaker only, and in mono. See Apple's support Web site for more information (docs.info.apple.com/article.html?artnum=93214).

STARTING A ONE-WAY VIDEO CHAT

Receiving a Video Chat

When someone invites you to a video chat, you have the option of accepting the invitation, declining it, or declining with a text message.

To receive a video chat:

◆ Click the Accept button to begin the video chat session (**Figure 7.13**).

◆ Click the Decline button to notify the other person that you don't want to participate (**Figure 7.14**).

◆ Click the Text Reply button to decline the chat but send a message using a text chat.

✔ Tips

■ iChat plays a ring sound when an incoming video chat invitation arrives, but plays it only once. To ensure that you don't miss it, go to iChat's Video preferences and select the checkbox labeled, "Play repeated ring sound when invited to a conference."

■ To configure the ring sound, or whether one plays at all, see Chapter 2.

■ To prevent others from inviting you to video chats, choose Camera Enabled from the Video menu to deselect that option. You'll need to turn it back on the next time you want to initiate a video chat.

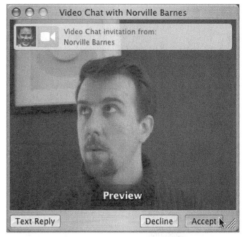

Figure 7.13 Click the Accept button or press the Return key to accept a video chat invitation.

Figure 7.14 That dastardly Norville declined my chat invitation. No ice cream for him!

Full Screen button

Full Screen mode

Figure 7.15 The Full Screen mode fills the entire area and hides system items such as the menu and Dock.

Figure 7.16 Moving your mouse pointer reveals the controls above the preview image in Full Screen mode.

Resizing the Video Window

The graphics technology in Mac OS X enables you to resize the video window, including the ability to view in Full Screen mode. The quality of the resized image depends upon the speed of your Internet connection and your Mac, but in most cases the picture is still quite usable.

To resize the video window:

Drag the resize handle in the lower-right corner of the window; the window resizes proportionally.

To view video full screen:

◆ Click the Full Screen button at the bottom of the chat window, or choose Full Screen from the Video menu. The image fills the entire screen (**Figure 7.15**).

◆ Click the Zoom button in the window's title bar, or choose Zoom from the Window menu.

To switch back to normal (windowed) mode:

◆ Press the Esc key.

   or

1. Move the mouse pointer to reveal the controls above the preview image (**Figure 7.16**).

2. Click the Full Screen button (which now appears with its arrows facing inward).

   You can also move the pointer to the top of the screen to reveal the menubar, then choose Full Screen from the View menu.

✔ Tip

■ The controls above the preview image in full-screen mode include a button marked with an X. This button ends the video chat entirely.

RESIZING THE VIDEO WINDOW

Muting and Pausing a Video Chat

As you're video chatting, you can mute the audio that gets sent to the other person, or pause your video (which also mutes the audio) while maintaining an active chat.

To mute audio:

Click the Mute button at the bottom of the chat window, or press the spacebar. The preview image indicates that audio is muted (**Figure 7.17**). You can still hear what the other person is saying.

To unmute, click the button or press the spacebar again.

To pause video and mute audio:

Choose Pause Video from the Video menu. The Pause icon in the preview image indicates that the outgoing audio and video feed is paused (**Figure 7.18**). You can still see and hear your buddy.

✔ Tips

- If you're using an iSight camera, turn the iris located around the lens assembly to pause your video chat.

- When your buddy mutes or pauses the chat, a Mute or Pause icon appears over the video feed to alert you.

Mute button

Figure 7.17 Muting the video feed stops sending audio to your buddy, though video continues.

Figure 7.18 Pausing the video freezes the outgoing video and audio feed.

Figure 7.19 Click and drag the preview image to reposition it within the chat window. The image snaps to a corner when you release it.

Preview image resize handle

Figure 7.20 The resize handle appears when you move your pointer over the preview image.

Arranging the Preview Image

The video chat window includes a picture-in-picture preview of what the other person sees in their window, so you can make sure your head is in the frame. This preview image can be resized or moved around at your convenience.

To position the preview image:

◆ Click a corner of the video chat window to snap the preview image to that location.

◆ Click and hold the center of the preview image (your mouse pointer becomes a grabber hand), then drag it to another corner of the window (**Figure 7.19**). Although you can drag it anywhere within the window, the preview jumps to a corner when you release the mouse button.

To resize the preview image:

1. Move the mouse pointer to the preview image to reveal the resize handle in the corner facing the middle of the window (**Figure 7.20**). In Full Screen mode, the handle appears with the controls above the preview image.

2. Drag the handle to shrink or enlarge the preview image. If you resize the chat window, the preview image also resizes proportionally.

Taking a Snapshot of a Video Chat

You can save single snapshots of a video chat for viewing later (or for blackmailing someone who likes to make funny faces on-camera).

To take a snapshot:

Choose Take Snapshot from the Video menu, or press Command-Option-S. A new image file is created on your Desktop (**Figure 7.21**).

✔ Tips

- iChat saves video snapshots as TIFF image files. To convert a snapshot to another format, such as JPEG, open the file in Preview and use the Export command located in the File menu.

- You can also take a picture clipping of an active video chat window. Command-click within the window, then drag to the Finder (**Figure 7.22**)—or drag it to the text field of an open text chat. This way, you can share video images even with someone who can't do video.

Figure 7.21 A snapshot of the video chat is saved to the Desktop. Here, I've opened the file in the Preview application.

Figure 7.22 Command-drag from the video chat window to create a picture clipping of that moment.

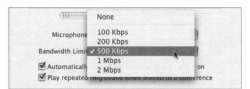

Figure 7.23 The Bandwidth Limit popup menu in the Video preferences helps control how much data iChat is attempting to send through your Net connection.

Figure 7.24 With the Bandwidth Limit set to 100 Kbps, top, there's more pixelation in the image, but potentially better performance overall. At 500 Kbps, bottom, there are fewer artifacts.

Setting Bandwidth Limit

Although bandwidth is often referred to in terms of speed, it's more accurate to talk about capacity. Bandwidth is like a pipe: the larger the pipe, the more data that can be passed through it.

In many cases, having a wider pipe is preferable—when more capacity is available, more data can be sent through the pipe. With video, that means you can send more image data, resulting in better performance and a clearer picture.

However, there are times when having a bandwidth surplus can be a detriment. iChat by default will use as much bandwidth as you can throw at it, because Apple wants you to see the best video image and hear the best audio quality. But using all that bandwidth could swamp your connection, which is bad news for other people on the network or if your ISP charges bandwidth surcharges for your Internet access. There are also times when iChat may try to use more bandwidth than is available.

For these occasions, you can change the amount of bandwidth that iChat uses. Shifting down to a lower bandwidth rate instructs iChat to apply more compression to the video and audio data, thereby taking up less bandwidth.

To set the bandwidth limit:

1. Open iChat's preferences, and click the Video icon.

2. Choose a speed from the Bandwidth Limit popup menu (**Figure 7.23**). 100 Kbps is less capacity than 2 Mbps (megabits per second) (**Figure 7.24**).

✔ Tip

- Changing the bandwidth limit is usually a good first troubleshooting step.

Mail and
File Transfer

Instant messaging works well for short,
pithy discussions, but email is still better for
longer memos and information that doesn't
demand an immediate response. You can
use iChat as a springboard for sending an
email message to anyone in your Buddy List.

On the flip side, instant messaging turns out
to be splendid for an un-message-like task:
transferring files from one person to another.

Sending Email from iChat

iChat looks to your system preferences to determine which email client you prefer. The method of setting the email client changed from Jaguar to Panther, so I've included both sequences below. You need to set this preference only once (unless you change email programs down the road).

To choose which email client to use (Mac OS X 10.3 Panther):

1. Launch Apple's Mail application.

2. Open Mail's preferences, and click the General icon.

3. Choose an email client from the Default Email Reader popup menu; you may need to choose Select to locate another application on your hard disk (**Figure 8.1**).

4. Close Mail's preferences.

To choose which email client to use (Mac OS X 10.2 Jaguar):

1. Open Mac OS X's preferences by choosing System Preferences under the Apple menu, or launching the System Preferences program in the Applications folder.

2. Click the Internet preference pane.

3. Click the Email tab.

4. From the Default Email Reader popup menu, choose an email client; you may need to choose Select to locate another application (**Figure 8.2**).

5. Close System Preferences.

Figure 8.1 For reasons known only to Apple, you must choose your default email client within the Mail application in Mac OS X 10.3 Panther.

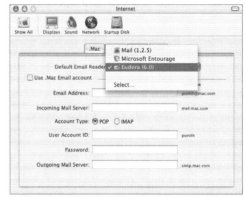

Figure 8.2 In Mac OS X 10.2 Jaguar, the default email client is specified in the Internet preference pane.

Figure 8.3 Specify the recipient of your email by choosing their name in the Participants drawer of a group chat.

Figure 8.4 In Mail, a new empty message is created, pre-addressed to the person you wish to send email.

To send email from iChat:

1. Choose the recipient of your email by performing one of the following actions:

   ▲ Select a person's name in the Buddy List.

   ▲ Bring an active chat window with the recipient to the front.

   ▲ If you're doing a group chat, select a buddy's name in the Participants drawer (**Figure 8.3**).

2. Choose Send Email from the Buddies menu, or press Command-Option-E. iChat switches to your preferred email application, where a new, pre-addressed outgoing message is ready (**Figure 8.4**).

✔ Tips

■ If you haven't specified an email address for a buddy, the Send Email command does not work (see Chapter 4 for instructions on adding information to a buddy's profile).

■ Select multiple buddies in the Buddy List or in a group chat and use Send Email to create a single message pre-addressed to all of them.

Checking Buddy Availability in Mail

If you were to look at my outgoing email, you'd see that most messages are short comments or questions that you'd find in a text chat. Wouldn't it be great if, when you need to ask a quick question of someone, you knew they were online? That way you could jump into iChat and ask away, rather than wait for a reply. Of course, you can.

To check buddy availability:

◆ Look at the messages in any mailbox. If a green indicator icon appears in the Buddy Availability column, the person who wrote the email is online (**Figure 8.5**).

◆ Look at individual messages. The green indicator icon appears beside the person's name if they're online (**Figure 8.6**).

To view the Buddy Availability column:

In Mail, go to the View menu, then the Columns submenu, and choose Buddy Availability. The column is active if a checkmark appears beside the name.

✔ Tips

■ Only buddies whose statuses are set to Available appear with the green indicator. Buddies who are logged into AIM but are either Idle or Away do not appear.

■ To move the Buddy Availability column (or any other column in Mail), click and hold the column's heading, and then drag it left or right to where you want it.

■ Mail normally sorts email messages based on their dates, but you can also sort according to availability. Choose Buddy Availability from the Sort By submenu of the View menu. Or, simply click the column heading in a mailbox; clicking it again reverses the sort order.

Buddy Availability indicator

Figure 8.5 The Buddy Availability column in the Mail application tells you when someone is logged in.

Buddy Availability indicator

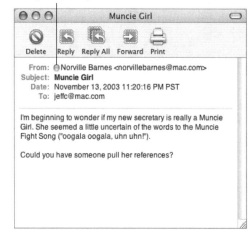

Figure 8.6 An indicator appears in the address fields of incoming or outgoing messages, regardless of when the email was written.

Double-click indicator to initiate chat.

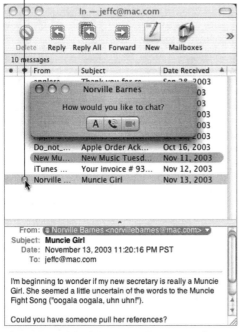

Figure 8.7 Double-clicking the indicator in Mail switches to iChat and asks which type of chat you'd like to start.

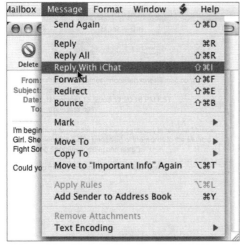

Figure 8.8 Use the Reply With iChat command in Mail to create a new chat with someone in iChat.

Starting a Chat from within Mail

You can initiate a chat directly from within Mail without manually switching to iChat and selecting your buddy.

To start a chat in Mail:

◆ Double-click the iChat indicator. iChat becomes the front-most application and a dialog appears for you to specify the type of chat (**Figure 8.7**).

◆ Choose Reply With iChat from the Message menu, or press Command-Shift-I. You can also choose Reply With iChat from the contextual menu (**Figure 8.8**). Choose a chat type in the dialog that appears.

✔ Tip

■ If the other person is only available to do a text chat (they don't have a camera or microphone, or they're using iChat 1.0), a new text chat window automatically appears in iChat when you double-click the indicator.

Transferring a File

People commonly send files to one another via email, which is fine for small things, but is problematic with large attachments—it puts a strain on the numerous email servers and Internet service providers that shuttle your boss's overblown PowerPoint presentation. Instead, send your file directly using iChat.

To send a file:

1. Do one of the following:

   ▲ Drag a file from the Finder to the name of a person in your Buddy List, to the text field of an open chat window, or to the name of a participant in a group chat (**Figure 8.9**).

   ▲ Select a person in your Buddy List or bring a chat window to the front, and choose Send File from the Buddies menu or press Command-Option-F.

2. A confirmation dialog appears (**Figure 8.10**). Click Send if you want to send the file. (Select the checkbox labeled "Don't ask again" to avoid this dialog in the future.)

3. Another dialog appears while iChat opens a connection and waits for the other person to accept the file transfer. If you want to abort, click the Stop button (**Figure 8.11**).

   When your buddy accepts, the file is sent.

✔ Tips

- You can send only one file at a time. To send a folder, compress it using an archive utility such as StuffIt (www.aladdinsys.com), or use the Create Archive feature of Mac OS X 10.3.

- Image and PDF files can be transferred, but they show up with previews in message windows (see "Sending and Receiving Images" in Chapter 5).

Figure 8.9 Drag a file from the Finder to a person in your Buddy List to transfer a file.

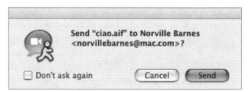

Figure 8.10 iChat verifies that you indeed want to send the file to the recipient.

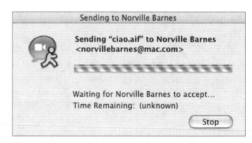

Figure 8.11 Once you've started the transfer process, the other person must accept it before the file is sent.

Figure 8.12 When someone sends a file, you can preview its type and size before accepting it.

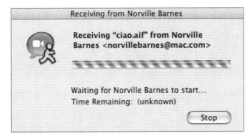

Figure 8.13 You see this dialog just prior to the file transfer. Click Stop to abort.

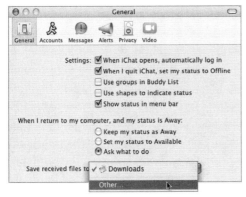

Figure 8.14 Go to iChat's General preferences to specify where received files are stored.

Receiving a File

When a buddy sends a file through iChat, you have the option of accepting or rejecting it.

To receive a file:

1. When a buddy sends a file, a new dialog appears (**Figure 8.12**). Click Save File to accept the file, or Decline to reject the transfer.

2. If you accept, you can click the Stop button during the download to abort the file transfer (**Figure 8.13**).

   iChat switches to the Finder when the transfer is complete, and selects the file in a new window.

To choose where downloaded files are saved:

1. Open iChat's preferences and click the General icon.

2. Click the popup menu labeled "Save received files to" and select Other (**Figure 8.14**).

3. In the save dialog that appears, specify a folder on your hard disk, then click OK.

✔ Tip

■ In Mac OS X 10.3 Panther, iChat determines where downloaded files are saved based on the preference in Safari. In Mac OS X 10.2 Jaguar, this preference appears in the Internet preference pane.

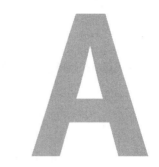

TROUBLESHOOTING

iChat succeeds as an instant-messaging application because it provides a simple, sensible interface for something that's actually quite complicated underneath. Encoding and transmitting video is a difficult and processor-intensive thing to do. (This helps explain why so many online video formats, such as Microsoft's Windows Media (WMV) or anything put out by RealNetworks—if I may editorialize briefly—tend to look and sound poor.) When you add the need to synchronize audio and video in real time with someone who can be anywhere on the globe, separated by innumerable combinations of network hardware and software, it's frankly amazing that it works at all sometimes.

But that's just it: sometimes it *doesn't* work. A file you transferred to one person won't go to another, or an audio connection that worked fine on Thursday won't stay active on Monday. Sometimes the problem can be solved at your end; sometimes it requires a system administrator; and sometimes, as happened to me recently, something at AOL or Apple went awry and messed up my .Mac account for several hours.

The following pages list some common troubleshooting situations and solutions, but it's not comprehensive. Be sure to check Apple's iChat support pages and discussion forums to stay up to date.

Where to Find Help

Apple's iChat support site

http://www.info.apple.com/usen/iChat/

Apple's iChat discussion forums

http://discussions.info.apple.com/

Apple telephone technical support

1-800-275-2273

Lost or Failed Connections

Perhaps the most common problem people run into is not being able to establish an audio or video connection with someone else. You may see an error message that says, "No data has been received for the last 10 seconds," or "There is insufficient bandwidth to maintain the connection," (**Figure A.1**). Try the following suggestions.

Check the Connection Doctor

1. Choose Connection Doctor from the Video menu.

2. Compare the Frame Rate values (**Figure A.2**) to see if the problem is originating at one end of the connection. Frame Rate measures the number of frames per second (fps) that iChat draws onscreen; a higher number represents smoother video animation. A good connection on a speedy Mac will get up to 30 fps, while a normal connection averages about 15 fps.

3. Check the Quality indicators to see if any data packets are being lost in transit from one machine to the other.

If the frame rate or quality indicators are low, try adjusting iChat's Bandwidth Limit setting.

Change the Bandwidth Limit setting

1. Open iChat's preferences and click the Video icon.

2. Choose a value from the Bandwidth Limit popup menu (**Figure A.3**).

3. If the connection is still active, the audio or video quality should improve. If the chat was dropped, attempt to reconnect to your buddy. (Your buddy may also need to adjust the Bandwidth Limit setting.)

Figure A.1 If iChat can't maintain a solid video connection, you may see an error such as this.

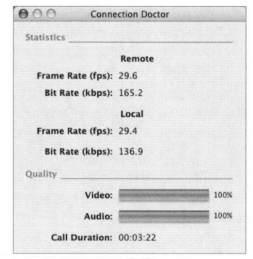

Figure A.2 The Connection Doctor provides real-time information about the status of your connection.

Figure A.3 The Bandwidth Limit popup menu in the Video preferences helps control how much data iChat is attempting to send through your Net connection.

Check your network connections

iChat can sometimes have trouble working over an AirPort Base Station, which uses 802.11b, or Wi-Fi, wireless networking. The newer AirPort Extreme Base Station, which uses faster 802.11g wireless networking, doesn't seem to have this problem. If you're using an AirPort Base Station, try connecting your Mac to a wired Ethernet connection. See `docs.info.apple.com/article.html?artnum=93218` for more information.

Check your firewall and NAT settings

Many networks today set up firewalls to prevent unauthorized access to its computers. Essentially, a firewall blocks all incoming or outgoing network traffic except for the data that you (or your system administrator) allow. These traffic points are called *ports*; iChat uses several ports for different kinds of traffic. For example, iChat uses port 5060 to signal and initiate chat invitations, while ports 16384 through 16403 are used to transfer video and audio data. If any of those ports are blocked, a connection cannot be made.

Network Address Translation (NAT) is a technology used by Internet Service Providers (ISPs) and some home networking routers to direct Internet traffic to machines on your network without assigning them each a unique Internet Protocol (IP) address.

So what does this mean in practical terms? First, make sure the firewall built into Mac OS X isn't blocking the ports you need (it's in the Sharing preference pane of Mac OS X's System Preferences). Second, you may need to contact your ISP or system administrator (if you're on a college campus or corporate network) and ask if the appropriate ports are open.

See `docs.info.apple.com/article.html?artnum=93208` for the specific technical information you'll need.

LOST OR FAILED CONNECTIONS

Check your Internet connection

Is your broadband connection operating with enough bandwidth to maintain an active video or audio chat? Although your ISP may claim that you're getting 256K connection speeds, that may not be a constant figure (especially with cable modems, which share bandwidth from a large pool; if all your neighbors also subscribe to cable Internet access, during peak times the bandwidth available to you is probably much less than optimal). To send and receive data, plus keep audio and video in sync, iChat performs continuous "handshaking" tasks to negotiate the connection. If the amount of available bandwidth is fluctuating, iChat may not be able to maintain the link.

The problem could also lie in the bandwidth rates for uploading and downloading data. If you subscribe to ADSL (Asynchronous DSL) service, the rate that data comes to you may be high, but the rate that data goes back to the Internet is likely much lower.

In any of the cases above, check with your ISP; they can determine the exact speeds that are available to your connection.

Chatting with Windows Users

iChat uses the AOL Instant Messaging (AIM) network to deliver text messages, images, and files. Your Windows-using buddy needs to have an active AIM account and the AIM software (download it at www.aim.com). See Chapter 4 for information on adding people to your Buddy List, and Chapter 5 for text chatting.

Currently, you can participate in audio and video chats only with other iChat users. Due to legal issues surrounding AOL's purchase of Time Warner in 2001, AOL was not permitted to incorporate videoconferencing in its instant messaging applications. That restriction has been lifted, in part due to iChat's appearance in the market, so I expect to see AIM video and audio chatting to be available sometime in 2004.

Also, iChat works only with the AIM network, which means friends using Microsoft's MSN Messenger (on Windows or Mac) can't chat with you. However, it is possible to chat with people who use the ICQ network: when adding a buddy, add their ICQ number in the screen name field. (Also note that they must be running the most recent version of the ICQ software, either for Mac or Windows.)

LOST OR FAILED CONNECTIONS

CUSTOMIZING iCHAT AV

B

Instant messaging. You type a message, you receive a message, you talk through a speaker or a camera—those are all nice applications, but isn't there some way to jazz up this simple little program?

Turns out there is. Enterprising developers have found ways to tweak the iChat interface, especially the status message, to make the chat experience a little richer.

Customizing iChat

Below are several software packages that extend the usefulness of iChat, or just make it more fun to use. Find more software at www.versiontracker.com.

Software Add-Ons

◆ **iChatStatus.** You can customize your status message in iChat for others to see something more interesting or descriptive than "Available" or "Away." iChatStatus makes the status message dynamic by listing the artist and song name of the track currently playing in iTunes (**Figure B.1**). (www.ittpoi.com)

◆ **Status Symbol.** Like iChatStatus, Status Symbol puts your iTunes music information into the message status line, but you can also configure it to display other information such as the local weather, stock quotes, a news ticker, and more (**Figure B.2**). (www.ifthensoft.com)

◆ **iChatter.** Text chat can be a silent affair, so give your words voice with iChatter, which lets you specify Mac OS speech voices to read text messages aloud as they come in. It's a fun change of pace, and no doubt helpful for sight-impaired users. (www.ecamm.com/mac/ichatter/)

◆ **iCal Calling iChat!** Using this custom AppleScript program, create a category in iCal called "iChat" and schedule items to be displayed in your status message for others to see. (www.malcolmadams.com/itunes/itinfo/icalcallingichatav.shtml)

◆ **Salling Clicker.** This isn't an iChat-specific program, but it boasts a nice iChat twist. If you own a Bluetooth-enabled cellular phone and have linked it to your Mac, Salling Clicker can automatically set your iChat status to "On the phone"

Figure B.1 iChatStatus lets the world in on your musical tastes, and frequently invites conversation.

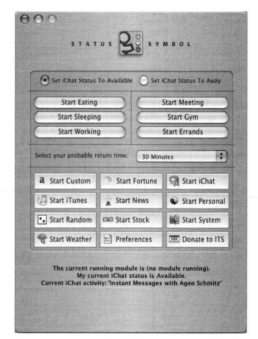

Figure B.2 Status Symbol offers more options for displaying information in the status message.

CUSTOMIZING iCHAT

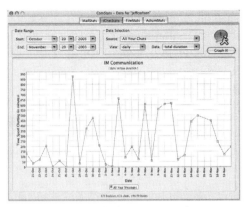

Figure B.3 ComStatus looks at your text chat transcripts to report on iChat (and Mail) usage.

Figure B.4 More iChat Smileys gives you 72 more emoticons.

when a call comes in or when you call someone else. When the call is complete, the status is reset to Available. It can also pause iTunes music playback when you're on the phone, plus dozens of other cool tricks (like controlling Keynote presentations from your cellular phone, or acting as a remote control when you watch DVDs on your computer). (homepage.mac.com/jonassalling/Shareware/Clicker/)

- ◆ **iChat Streaming Icon.** If a static buddy icon is too boring for you, this application sends multiple video snapshots of you to approximate a live video feed as your icon. People who have you in their buddy lists will not only see that you're at your computer, but watch you move as well. (www.apple.com/downloads/macosx/email_chat/ichatstreamingicon.html)

- ◆ **ComStats.** How much time do you spend using iChat? Find out exactly, with graphs, using ComStats (**Figure B.3**). It analyzes your text chat transcripts to generate a report on how often you chat, and more. (www.instituteofthefuture.org/comstats/)

- ◆ **More iChat Smileys.** If 16 smiley icons aren't enough for you, install this extended set of 72 more. Your buddies also need to install the software to see the new smileys. (www.lemacenligne.com)

Online iChat Communities

Are your friends all stuck using PCs? Or are you simply interested in meeting new people online? A few iChat communities have sprung up where sociable people hook up and chat with one another.

- ◆ **iChat Finder** (www.ichatfinder.com)

- ◆ **iChattin'** (www.ichattin.com)

- ◆ **My iSight** (www.myisight.com)

CUSTOMIZING iCHAT

INDEX

@ (atmark symbol), 20

A

Accept button, 51, 75, 86
accounts
    adding buddies to Buddy List, 32, 33
    adding new accounts, 22
    AIM accounts, 10, 22
    creating a persona, 11
    iChat screen names, 10
    logging in and out, 22, 23
    .Mac accounts, 10, 22
    switching between accounts, 22
Accounts preferences, 22
Acronym Dictionary, AOL, 56
acronyms, common, 56
actions
    alert actions, 20
    buddy-specific actions, 42–43
    for single event, specifying, 43
Actions option, Show popup menu, 42
Add Buddy option, Buddies menu, 32, 33
Add Hyperlink option, Edit menu, 61
Address Book
    adding buddies to Buddy List, 33, 34
    initiating chats, 36
    status indicators, 36
    storing multiple screen names, 36
    viewing buddy information, 36
Adobe Photoshop, 29
ADS Tech, 80
AIM accounts
    adding buddies to Buddy List, 32, 33
    chatting with Windows users, 104
    iChat screen names, 10
    logging in and out, 22, 23
    switching between accounts, 22

AIM network, 6. *See also* AIM accounts
AIM profiles, adding, 41
AirPort Base Station, 103
alerts
    alert actions, 20
    buddy-specific actions, 42–43
    repeating, 20, 86
    sounds, adding and removing, 21
Alerts preferences, 20
Allow Anyone (privacy level), 24
Allow People in my Buddy List
        (privacy level), 24
Allow Specific People (privacy level), 24
Always use this picture (check box), 40
AOL accounts, 10. *See also* AIM accounts
AOL Instant Messaging. *See* AIM network
atmark symbol (@), 20
audible alerts
    alert actions, 20, 75
    sounds, adding and removing, 21
Audio Chat button, 71, 72
audio chat window
    minimizing, 73
    overview, 4
    sound level indicator, 72
    volume control slider, 72
audio chats
    buddy's audio capability, determining, 71
    call duration, 73
    Connection Doctor, 77, 102
    full-duplex audio technology, 69, 72
    initiating, 72, 74
    iTunes and, 73
    microphone source setting, 70
    muting outgoing audio, 76
    one-way audio chats, 74
    preventing others from initiating, 75
    receiving, 75
    speakers, sound quality of, 70, 73, 84
    system requirements, 2, 70
    troubleshooting audio quality, 76
    troubleshooting connections, 77, 102–104
    troubleshooting microphones, 71
    window (*See* audio chat window)
audio input source, setting, 70
audio level indicator, 4, 5, 72, 82
Audio menu, Enable Microphone option, 75
Audio Status button, 72
audio status icons, 38, 71, 72
automated chat software (chat bots), 53
Available status
    checking availability from Mail, 96
    setting status, 12
    sorting Buddy List by status, 39

Away status
    receiving chats, 13
    setting status, 12
    sorting Buddy List by status, 39
    text chat etiquette guidelines, 56

B

802.11b wireless network connections, 103
background, setting, 18–19
balloons, text chat
    changing balloon color, 16
    changing text color, 16, 63
    displaying text blocks instead, 17, 64
    formatting text, 16, 63
bandwidth
    iChat bandwidth requirements, 91, 104
    setting bandwidth limit, 91, 102
bit rate statistics, 77
Block button, 51, 52
Block Everyone (privacy level), 24, 53
Block Specific People (privacy level), 24, 52, 53
blocking chats
    blocking specific people, 24, 52
    privacy levels, 24
    unblocking people, 53
blocks, displaying instead of balloons, 17, 64
bold text in text chats, 63
bots (chat bots), 53
Bounce icon in the Dock action, 20, 42
broadband Internet connections
    bandwidth and bandwidth limits, 91, 102, 104
    iChat requirements, 81, 104
browsing chat transcripts, 66–67
buddies. *See also* buddy icons; Buddy List
    adding to Buddy List, 32–35
    AIM profiles, 41
    availability, 12, 39, 96
    buddy actions, 42–43
    groups. *See* buddy groups
    identification options in message
        windows, 64
    notes, in Info dialog, 41
    removing from Buddy List, 34, 35
    selecting in Buddy List, 35
    viewing buddy information, 36, 40–41
Buddies menu
    Add Buddy option, 32, 33
    Get Info option, 33, 40
    Invite to Chat option, 54
    Invite to One-Way Audio Chat option, 74
    Invite to One-Way Video Chat option, 85
    Send Direct Message option, 49
    Send Email option, 37, 95

Send File option, 98
Send Instant Message option, 48
Show in Address Book option, 36
Buddy Availability column, Mail, 96
buddy groups
    adding buddies, 45
    creating, 44
    enabling and disabling, 44
    removing buddies, 45
    removing groups, 46
    viewing groups, 46
buddy icons. *See also* buddies; images
    adding buddies to Buddy List, 32, 34
    buddy identification options, message
        windows, 64
    changing in Info dialog, 40
    clearing icons, 30
    cropping images, 26, 29
    displayed in Buddy List, 4, 38
    editing images, 29
    finding images, 26, 27
    image resolution, 29
    resizing images, 29
    sharpening images, 29
    switching between icons, 30
    using imported images, 26–27
    using multiple icons, 30
    using streaming video feed, 28, 107
    using video capture, 28
Buddy List. *See also* buddies
    adding buddies, 32–35
    audio status, determining, 38, 71, 72
    buddy icons, displaying, 38
    customizing display, 38–39
    editing address information, 33
    initiating chats, 48–49, 72, 84
    multiple screen names, storing, 37
    offline buddies, displaying, 38
    overview, 31
    removing buddies, 35, 36
    selecting buddies, 35
    sort options, 39
    storage location, 35
    video status, determining, 38, 72, 83
    viewing buddy information, 36, 40–41
Buddy Picture dialog. *See also* buddy icons
    cropping images, 26
    finding images, 26, 27
    taking video snapshots, 28

C

call duration, 73, 77
camcorders. *See also* video cameras

DV camcorders, 80, 81
    iChat requirements, 80
Camera Enabled option, Video menu, 81, 86
cameras. *See* video cameras
Change My Picture option, 26
chat bots, 53
chat transcripts, 66–67
chat windows
    audio chat window, 4, 72, 73
    background images, 18–19
    Buddy List. *See* Buddy List
    minimizing windows, 5, 73
    switching between windows, 5
    text chat window. *See* message windows
    video chat window. *See* video chat window
    zooming windows, 5
chats
    audio. *See* audio chats
    blocking, 24, 52, 53
    cross-platform chatting, 104
    ending, 50, 84, 87
    initiating. *See* initiating chats
    receiving. *See* receiving chats
    text. *See* text chats
    video. *See* video chats
Check Spelling as You Type option, 58, 59
checking spelling, 58–59
circle status indicator, 13
Clear Background option, View menu, 18, 19
Clear Recent Pictures option, 30
clippings of video windows, 90
closing chats
    text chats, 50
    video chats, 84, 87
color
    balloon color, 16
    chat background, 19
    formatting incoming messages, 65
    text block color, 17, 64
    text color, 16, 63
communities online, iChat, 107
ComStats, 107
Connection Doctor, 77, 102
connections
    bandwidth, requirements and
        limits, 91, 102, 104
    bit rate statistics, 77
    call duration statistics, 77
    Connection Doctor, 77, 102
    data loss statistics, 77, 102
    diagnostics and troubleshooting, 77, 102–104
    firewall settings, 103
    frame rate statistics, 102
    Internet connection settings, 104

connections, *continued*
  NAT settings, 103
  wireless network connections, 103
controlling who can send messages
  blocking specific people, 24, 52
  privacy levels, 24
  unblocking people, 53
copying buddies to groups, 45
cross-platform chatting, 104
Custom option, status popup menu, 14
custom status messages, 14–15, 106

D

data loss statistics, 77, 102
Decline button, 51, 75, 86
diagnostics. *See* troubleshooting
direct messages, 48, 49, 62. *See also* text chat
discussion forums, iChat, 101
dot Mac. *See* .Mac accounts
downloading files, 99
DV camcorders, 80, 81

E

Ecamm Network, 80
Edit menu
  Add Hyperlink option, 61
  Insert Smiley submenu, 60
Edit Status Menu option, status popup
    menu, 15
editing text before sending, 50
email
  sending from iChat, 37, 95
  specifying email client, 94
email addresses as screen names, 10
emoticons (smileys), 60, 107
Enable Microphone option, Audio menu, 75
End Chat button, 84
ending chats
  text chats, 50
  video chats, 84, 87
etiquette guidelines, text chats, 56
events
  setting alerts, 20, 21
  setting buddy-specific actions, 42–43
exiting chats. *See* ending chats
eye contact in video chats, 83

F

File menu, New Chat with Person option, 49
files
  chat transcripts, 66–67

saving, 99
  transferring and receiving, 98–99
Fire-I, 80
firewalls, 103
first names, sorting Buddy List, 39
fluorescent lighting, 82
fonts
  incoming message formatting, 65
  outgoing message formatting, 16, 63
  text chat etiquette guidelines, 56
frame rate statistics, 102
full-duplex audio technology, 69, 72
Full Screen button, 5, 87
Full Screen mode, 84, 87
Full Screen option, View menu, 87

G

General preferences
  folder location for received files, 99
  logging in automatically, 23
  setting status automatically, 12
  status indicator shapes, 13
Get Info option, Buddies menu, 33, 40
GraphicConverter, 29
graphics. *See also* buddy icons
  changing buddy's icon, 40
  chat background, setting, 18–19
  clippings of video chats, 90
  cropping images, 26, 29
  editing images, 29
  finding images, 26, 27
  image resolution, 29
  importing images, 26, 27
  resizing images, 29
  sending and receiving files, 98–99
  sending and receiving images, 62, 90
  sharpening images, 29
  smileys, 60, 107
  snapshots of video chats, 90
  video captures, 28
  zooming in, 29
green circle status indicator, 13
green status indicator, 12
group chats. *See also* text chats
  adding people, 55
  ignoring participants, 56
  initiating, 54, 57
  inviting participants, 54, 55
  joining, 57
  public group chats, 57
  sending email from iChat, 95
  showing and hiding participants, 56

groups. *See* buddy groups; group chats
Groups drawer, 44, 45, 46

H

Hamlet, 50, 54, 60
headphones, 70
Henry V, 63, 64
hyperlinks in chats, 61

I

iBot, 80
iCal Calling iChat, 106
iChat
　availability, 2
　chatting with Windows users, 104
　iChat, iChat 1.0, and iChat AV, 3
　initial setup, 11
　interface, 4–5
　ports used by, 103
　system requirements, 2–3, 70, 80–81
iChat 1.0. *See* iChat
iChat accounts. *See also* accounts
　adding new accounts, 22
　creating a persona, 11
　logging in and out, 22
　switching between accounts, 22
iChat AV. *See* iChat
iChat communities online, 107
iChat discussion forums, Apple, 101
iChat Finder, 107
iChat menu bar icon, 5
iChat screen names. *See* screen names
iChat Streaming Icon, 28, 107
iChat support site, Apple, 101
iChatStatus, 15, 106
iChatter, 106
iChattin', 107
iChatUSBCam, 80
icons. *See also* status indicators
　audio status icons, 38, 71, 72
　buddy icons. *See* buddy icons
　emoticons (smileys), 60, 107
　iChat icon, bouncing, 20, 42
　iChat menu bar icon, 5
　status indicator shapes, displaying, 13
　video status icons, 38, 72, 83, 84
ICQ network users, 104
identities. *See also* accounts
　adding new accounts, 22
　creating, 11
　switching between accounts, 22
Idle status

blocking display of, 13
　setting status, 12
　sorting Buddy List by status, 39
images. *See also* buddy icons
　changing buddy's icon, 40
　chat background, setting, 18–19
　clippings of video chats, 90
　cropping, 26, 29
　editing, 29
　finding pictures, 26, 27
　importing, 26, 27
　resizing, 29
　resolution of images, 29
　sending and receiving, 62, 90
　sending and receiving files, 98–99
　sharpening, 29
　smileys, 60, 107
　snapshots of video chats, 90
　zooming in, 29
iMic, 70
incoming chats
　adding new buddies to Buddy List, 33
　blocking chats from specific people, 24, 52
　iChat menu bar icon, 5
　receiving chats, 51, 75, 86
　unblocking people, 53
indicators. *See* status indicators
Info dialog
　adding notes, 41
　adding profile information, 42
　assigning buddy actions, 42–43
　Capabilities list, 71, 83
　changing buddy's icon, 40
initiating chats
　from Address Book, 36
　audio chats, 72
　chat bots, 53
　direct messages, 48, 49
　group chats, 54
　instant messages, 48
　from Mail, 97
　with someone not in Buddy List, 49
　text chats, 48–49
　video chats, 84
instant messages, 6, 7, 48, 62. *See also* text chat
Internet connections
　AIM network, 6
　audio chat requirements, 2, 70
　bandwidth, requirements and
　　limits, 91, 102, 104
　Connection Doctor, 77, 102
　frame rate statistics, 102
　text chat requirements, 2
　video chat requirements, 3, 81

invitations to group chats, 54, 55.
See also initiating chats
Invite to Audio Chat option, 71, 72
Invite to Chat option, Buddies menu, 54
Invite to One-Way Audio Chat option, 74
Invite to One-Way Video Chat option, 85
Invite to Video Chat option, 83, 84
iSight camera
   My iSight, 107
   pausing video feed, 88
   video chat requirements, 3, 80
italic text, in text chats, 63
iTunes
   and audio chats, 73
   listing in status messages, 15, 106

J

JPEG files, 90

K

keyboard shortcuts
   adding buddies, 32, 33
   checking spelling, 58, 59
   editing address information, 33
   editing text, 50
   initiating chats, 48, 49
   logging in using Rendezvous, 7
   selecting buddies, 35
   sending direct messages, 49
   sending email from iChat, 37, 95
   sending instant messages, 48
   switching between windows, 5
   taking video snapshots, 90
   viewing buddy information, 40

L

laptop speakers, 70, 73, 84
last names, sorting Buddy List, 39
latency, 81
lighting levels, 82
local networks. *See* Rendezvous messaging
logging in and out
   AIM accounts, 22, 23
   logging in automatically, 23
   .Mac accounts, 22
   using Rendezvous, 7
Logorrhea, 67
logs of text chats, 66–67

M

.Mac accounts
   adding buddies to Buddy List, 32, 33
   creating a persona, 11
   iChat screen names, 10
   logging in, 22
   switching between accounts, 22
mac.com email addresses, 10
Mail
   Buddy Availability column, 96
   sending email from iChat, 37, 95
   specifying email client, 94
   starting chats from Mail, 97
menu. *See* iChat menu bar icon
message windows. *See also* text chats
   buddy identification options, 64
   exiting chats, 50
   message appearance options, 16, 17, 63, 64
   receiving text chats, 51
   sending direct messages, 49
   sending instant messages, 48
   text chat window overview, 4
   text formatting, 16, 63, 65
messages
   chats. *See* text chats
   email. *See* email; Mail
   status. *See* status messages
Messages preferences
   balloon color, 16
   colored text blocks, 17
   fonts, 16
   formatting incoming messages, 65
   saving chat transcripts, 66–67
   text color, 16
microphones
   audio chat requirements, 2, 70
   audio input source, setting, 70
   disabling, 75
   iMic, 70
   iSight, 70
   sound level indicator, 72, 82
   troubleshooting, 71
   video chat requirements, 3
Minimize button, 5
minimizing windows, 5
More iChat Smileys, 107
motion, in video chats, 85
MSN Messenger users, 104
Mute button, 4, 5, 6, 76, 88
muting outgoing audio, 76, 88
My iSight, 107

N

names. *See also* screen names
  adding buddies to Buddy List, 32, 33, 34
  buddy identification options, message
    windows, 64
  removing buddies from Buddy List, 34, 35
  sorting Buddy List, 39
NAT (Network Address Translation), 103
networking. *See also* connections
  AIM network, 6
  Rendezvous messaging, 7
New Chat with Person option, File menu, 49
notes, in Info dialog, 41

O

Offline status
  blocking specific people, 52
  displaying in Buddy List, 38
  receiving chats, 23
  setting status, 13
on-the-fly custom status messages, 14, 15
"On the phone" status, 106–107
one-way audio chats, 74
one-way video chats, 85
online discussion forums, Apple iChat, 101
online iChat communities, 107
operating system requirements
  audio chat, 2
  text chat, 2
  video chat, 3, 80
Orange Micro, 80
orange triangle status indicator, 13

P

packet loss statistics, 77, 102
Participants drawer, 55, 56
participants in group chats
  adding to chat in progress, 55
  ignoring people, 56
  inviting, 54, 55
  public group chats, 57
  showing and hiding, 56
Pause Video option, Video menu, 88
pausing outgoing video, 88
PDFs, sending and receiving files, 98–99
personas. *See also* accounts
  adding new accounts, 22
  creating, 11
  switching between accounts, 22
Picard, Jean-Luc, 83
picture clippings of video windows, 90

pictures. *See also* buddy icons
  changing buddy's icon, 40
  chat background, setting, 18–19
  clippings of video chats, 90
  cropping, 26, 29
  editing, 29
  finding images, 26, 27
  image resolution, 29
  importing, 26, 27
  resizing images, 29
  sending and receiving files, 98–99
  sending and receiving images, 62, 90
  sharpening images, 29
  smileys, 60, 107
  snapshots of video chats, 90
  zooming in, 29
Play sound action, 20, 21, 42
plus-sign (+), Buddy List, 32, 33
ports used by iChat, 103
preferences
  adding accounts, 22
  alerts, 20
  balloon color, 16
  bandwidth limit, 91, 102
  blocking or allowing people, 24, 52, 53
  chat transcripts, 66–67
  colored text blocks, 17
  email client, 94
  folder location for received files, 99
  fonts, 16
  formatting incoming messages, 65
  Idle status, blocking display of, 13
  logging in automatically, 23
  microphone source, 70
  opening iChat when camera is turned on, 81
  previewing video feed, 81
  privacy levels, 24
  setting status automatically, 12
  status indicator shapes, 13
  switching between accounts, 22
  text color, 16
preventing chat invitations
  audio chats, 75
  blocking specific people, 24, 52
  privacy levels, 24
  unblocking people, 53
  video chats, 86
previewing video feed
  adjusting lighting, 82
  positioning preview image, 89
  in preview window, 82
  resizing preview image, 89
  in Video preferences window, 81

Privacy preferences
blocking or allowing people, 24, 52, 53
Idle status, blocking display of, 13
privacy levels, 24
processor requirements
audio chat, 2
text chat, 2
video chat, 3, 80
profiles, AIM, 41
public group chats, 57. *See also* group chats
Pyro 1394 WebCam, 80

Q

Quality area, Connection Doctor, 77, 102
quitting chats
text chats, 50
video chats, 84, 87

R

receiving chats
adding new buddies to Buddy List, 33
audio chats, 75
blocking chats from specific people, 24, 52
iChat menu bar icon, 5
message window buttons, 51
Offline status, 23
privacy levels, 24
text chats, 51
unblocking people, 53
video chats, 86
receiving files, 99
red square status indicator, 13
red status indicator, 12
Remember custom messages (check box), 15
removing
buddies from buddy groups, 45
buddies from Buddy List, 34, 35
buddy groups, 46
custom status messages, 15
sounds, 21
Rendezvous messaging. *See also* AIM network
direct messages, 49
editing text, 50
enabling, 7
logging in, 7
overview, 7
repeating alerts, 20, 86
Reply with iChat option, Mail, 97
resizing
images, 29
preview image, 89
video window, 87

S

Salling Clicker, 106–107
satellite Internet connections, 81
saving
chat transcripts, 66
downloaded files, 99
screen names
adding buddies to Buddy List, 32, 33
adding new accounts, 22
AIM accounts, 10
buddy identification options, message
windows, 64
initiating chats, 49
.Mac accounts, 10
multiple screen names, storing, 37
removing buddies from Buddy List, 34, 35
switching between accounts, 22
Send Direct Message option, Buddies menu, 49
Send Email option, Buddies menu, 37, 95
Send File option, Buddies menu, 98
Send Instant Message option, Buddies menu, 48
Send text as I type (Rendezvous only)
(check box), 50
sending files, 98
Set Chat Background option, View menu, 18, 19
sharpening images, 29
Show as Balloons option, View menu, 64
Show as Text option, View menu, 64, 65
Show Audio Status option, View menu, 38, 71
Show Buddy Pictures option, View menu, 38
Show in Address Book option, Buddies menu, 36
Show Names and Pictures option,
View menu, 64
Show Names option, View menu, 64, 65
Show Pictures option, View menu, 64
Show Video Status option, View menu, 38, 83
Smiley popup menu, 4
smileys, 60, 107
snapshots of video chats, 90
software add-ons
ComStats, 107
iCal Calling iChat, 106
iChat Streaming Icon, 28, 107
iChatStatus, 15, 106
iChatter, 106
More iChat Smileys, 107
Salling Clicker, 106–107
Status Symbol, 106
Sort by Availability option, View menu, 39
Sort by First Name option, View menu, 39
Sort by Last Name option, View menu, 39
sort options, Buddy List, 39
sound level indicator, 72, 82

INDEX

sounds
  adding and removing, 21
  alert actions, 20, 75
Speak text action, 20, 43
speakers
  audio chat requirements, 70
  sound quality of, 70, 73, 84
Spelling dialog, 58–59
square status indicator, 13
statistics
  iChat usage statistics, 107
  Statistics area, Connection Doctor, 77, 102
status
  changing, 12
  checking from Mail, 96
  displayed in Buddy List, 4, 12
  indicators. *See* status indicators
  messages. *See* status messages
  setting automatically, 12
  sorting Buddy List by status, 39
status indicators
  in Address Book, 36
  in Buddy List, 4, 12
  iChat menu bar icon, 5
  shapes, displaying instead of spheres, 13
status messages
  custom messages, 14–15, 106
  displayed in Buddy List, 4, 12
  displaying iCal schedule items, 106
  listing current iTune, 15, 106
  "On the phone" status, 106–107
status popup menu
  in Buddy List window, 4
  Custom option, 14
  Edit Status Menu option, 15
  setting status, 12
Status Symbol, 106
streaming video as buddy icon, 28, 107
support Web sites, iChat, 101
switching between accounts, 22
switching between buddy icons, 30
switching between windows, 5
system requirements
  audio chat, 2, 70
  text chat, 2
  video chat, 3, 80–81

T

Take Snapshot option, Video menu, 90
Take Video Snapshot button, 28
technical support. *See also* troubleshooting iChat
  Apple telephone support, 101
  discussion forums, iChat, 101

iChat support Web sites, Apple, 101
text
  changing color, 16, 63
  changing font, 16, 63
  displaying colored text blocks, 17, 64
  editing before sending, 50
  formatting incoming text, 65
  formatting outgoing text, 16, 63
text chat window, 4, 18–19
text chats
  acronyms, common, 56
  balloon color, 16
  buddy identification options, 64
  checking spelling, 58–59
  colored text blocks, 17, 64
  direct messages, 48, 49
  editing text, 50
  etiquette guidelines, 56
  exiting chats, 50
  formatting text, 16, 63, 65
  group chats, 54–57
  hyperlinks, 61
  images, sending and receiving, 62
  initiating, 48–49
  instant messages, 48
  message display options, 16–17, 63, 64, 65
  public group chats, 57
  receiving, 51
  smileys (emoticons), 60, 107
  speech voices, specifying, 106
  system requirements, 2
  transcripts, 66–67
text entry field, 4
Text Reply button, 75, 86
transcripts, 66–67
transferring files, 98
triangle status indicator, 13
troubleshooting iChat
  audio quality, 76
  bandwidth requirements and
    limits, 91, 102, 104
  Connection Doctor, 77, 102
  connections, 77, 102–104
  DV camcorders, 81
  iChat discussion forums, Apple, 101
  iChat support Web site, Apple, 101
  microphone recognition, 71
  video camera recognition, 81
  video connections, 102–104
  Windows users, chatting with, 104
  wireless network connections, 103
typing text
  checking spelling, 58–59
  editing text, 50

typing text, *continued*
    etiquette guidelines, text chats, 56
    formatting options, 16, 63, 65
    hyperlinks, 61
    initiating text chats, 48, 49
    sending text while typing, 50
    smileys (emoticons), 60, 107

U

underlined text, in text chats, 63
Unibrain, 80
URLs, inserting in chats, 61
USB webcams, 80
utilities
    ComStats, 107
    iCal Calling iChat, 106
    iChat Streaming Icon, 28, 107
    iChatStatus, 15, 106
    iChatter, 106
    More iChat Smileys, 107
    Salling Clicker, 106–107
    Status Symbol, 106

V

video cameras
    connecting, 81
    streaming video feed, as buddy icon, 28, 107
    troubleshooting video camera recognition, 81
    video capture, as buddy icon, 28
    video chat requirements, 3, 80, 81
Video Chat button, 83, 84
video chat window
    Full Screen mode, 84, 87
    one-way video chats, 85
    overview, 5
    positioning, 83
    previewing video feed, 81, 82
    resizing, 87
    taking snapshots or clippings, 90
video chats
    bandwidth requirements and
        limits, 91, 102, 104
    buddy's video capability, determining, 83
    clippings, saving, 90
    ending, 84, 87
    eye contact, 83
    initiating, 84
    motion, excessive, 85
    muting outgoing audio, 88
    one-way video chat, 85
    pausing outgoing video, 88
    preventing others from initiating, 86

    receiving, 86
    snapshots, saving, 90
    system requirements, 3, 80–81
    window. *See* video chat window
video feed
    adjusting lighting, 82
    previewing, 81, 82
    using for buddy icon, 28, 107
Video menu
    Camera Enabled option, 81, 86
    Pause Video option, 88
    Take Snapshot option, 90
Video preferences
    bandwidth limit, 91, 102
    microphone source, 70
    opening iChat when camera is turned on, 81
    previewing video feed, 81
video status icons
    determining buddy's video status, 83
    dimmed, 72
    displaying, 38
    initiating video chat, 84
View menu
    Clear Background option, 18, 19
    Full Screen option, 87
    Set Chat Background option, 18, 19
    Show as Balloons option, 64
    Show as Text option, 64, 65
    Show Audio Status option, 38, 71
    Show Buddy Pictures option, 38
    Show Names and Pictures option, 64
    Show Names option, 64, 65
    Show Pictures option, 64
    Show Video Status option, 38, 83
    Sort by Availability option, 39
    Sort by First Name option, 39
    Sort by Last Name option, 39
visible alerts, 20
volume slider control, 4, 5, 72

W

Web addresses
    Acronym Dictionary, AOL, 56
    Adobe Photoshop, 29
    ADS Tech, 80
    AIM Web site, 10
    ComStats, 107
    Ecamm Network, 80
    Fire-I, 80
    GraphicConverter, 29
    Griffin Technology, 70
    iBot, 80
    iCal Calling iChat, 106

INDEX

iChat discussion forums, Apple, 101
iChat Finder, 107
iChat Streaming Icon, 28, 107
iChat support site, Apple, 101
iChatStatus, 106
iChatter, 106
iChattin', 107
iChatUSBCam, 80
iMic, 70
iSight, 80
laptop speaker quality, Apple support
    information, 73, 84
Logorrhea, 67
.Mac accounts, 10
More iChat Smileys, 107
My iSight, 107
online iChat communities, 107
Orange Micro, 80
Pyro 1394 WebCam, 80
Rendezvous, 7
Salling Clicker, 107
Status Symbol, 106
TidBITS, 54
Unibrain, 80
Unofficial Smiley Dictionary, 60
webcams. *See also* video cameras
    USB webcams, 80
    video chat system requirements, 80
windows
    audio chat window, 4
    background images, 18–19
    Buddy List, 4
    minimizing windows, 5
    switching between windows, 5
    text chat window, 4
    video chat window, 5, 83, 85, 87
    zooming windows, 5
Windows users, chatting with, 104

Y

yellow status indicator, 12

Z

Zoom button, 5, 87
zooming
    cropping images, 29
    full-screen video mode, 87
    windows, 5